W9-DJB-259

ROBERT
FROST

Other titles in the Greenhaven Press Literary Companion Series:

American Authors

Maya Angelou
Stephen Crane
Emily Dickinson
William Faulkner
F. Scott Fitzgerald
Nathaniel Hawthorne
Ernest Hemingway
Herman Melville
Arthur Miller
Eugene O'Neill
Edgar Allan Poe
John Steinbeck
Mark Twain
Walt Whitman
Thornton Wilder

American Literature

The Adventures of Huckleberry Finn
The Adventures of Tom Sawyer
The Call of the Wild
The Catcher in the Rye
The Crucible
Death of a Salesman
The Glass Menagerie
The Grapes of Wrath
The Great Gatsby
Of Mice and Men
The Old Man and the Sea
The Pearl
The Scarlet Letter
A Separate Peace

British Authors

Jane Austen
Joseph Conrad
Charles Dickens

British Literature

Animal Farm
Beowulf
Brave New World
The Canterbury Tales
Great Expectations
Hamlet
Heart of Darkness
Julius Caesar
Lord of the Flies
Macbeth
Pride and Prejudice
Romeo and Juliet
Shakespeare: The Comedies
Shakespeare: The Histories
Shakespeare: The Sonnets
Shakespeare: The Tragedies
A Tale of Two Cities
Wuthering Heights

World Authors

Fyodor Dostoyevsky
Homer
Sophocles

World Literature

Antigone
All Quiet on the Western Front
The Diary of a Young Girl
A Doll's House

THE GREENHAVEN PRESS
Literary Companion
TO AMERICAN AUTHORS

READINGS ON

ROBERT FROST

Andrea DeFusco, *Book Editor*

David L. Bender, *Publisher*
Bruno Leone, *Executive Editor*
Bonnie Szumski, *Series Editor*

Greenhaven Press, Inc., San Diego, CA

Every effort has been made to trace the owners of copyrighted material. The articles in this volume may have been edited for content, length, and/or reading level. The titles have been changed to enhance the editorial purpose. Those interested in locating the original source will find the complete citation on the first page of each article.

Library of Congress Cataloging-in-Publication Data

Readings on Robert Frost / Andrea DeFusco, book editor.
    p.   cm. — (The Greenhaven Press literary
companion to American authors)
    Includes bibliographical references and index.
    ISBN 1-56510-998-8 (pbk. : alk. paper). —
ISBN 1-56510-999-6 (lib. : alk. paper)
    1. Frost, Robert, 1874–1963—Criticism and interpretation. I. Title. II. Series.
PS3511.R94Z6145   1999
811'.52—dc21
                                                                98-48267
                                                                CIP

Cover photo: AP/Wide World

Copyright ©1999 by Greenhaven Press, Inc.
PO Box 289009
San Diego, CA 92198-9009
Printed in the U.S.A.

"I'm going out to clean the pasture spring;
I'll only stop to rake the leaves away
(And wait to watch the water clear, I may):
I shan't be gone long.—You come too.

I'm going out to fetch the little calf
That's standing by the mother. It's so young
It totters when she licks it with her tongue.
I shan't be gone long.—You come too."

—Robert Frost, "The Pasture"

CONTENTS

FOREWORD

"'Tis the good reader that
makes the good book."

Ralph Waldo Emerson

The story's bare facts are simple: The captain, an old and scarred seafarer, walks with a peg leg made of whale ivory. He relentlessly drives his crew to hunt the world's oceans for the great white whale that crippled him. After a long search, the ship encounters the whale and a fierce battle ensues. Finally the captain drives his harpoon into the whale, but the harpoon line catches the captain about the neck and drags him to his death.

A simple story, a straightforward plot—yet, since the 1851 publication of Herman Melville's *Moby-Dick*, readers and critics have found many meanings in the struggle between Captain Ahab and the whale. To some, the novel is a cautionary tale that depicts how Ahab's obsession with revenge leads to his insanity and death. Others believe that the whale represents the unknowable secrets of the universe and that Ahab is a tragic hero who dares to challenge fate by attempting to discover this knowledge. Perhaps Melville intended Ahab as a criticism of Americans' tendency to become involved in well-intentioned but irrational causes. Or did Melville model Ahab after himself, letting his fictional character express his anger at what he perceived as a cruel and distant god?

Although literary critics disagree over the meaning of *Moby-Dick*, readers do not need to choose one particular interpretation in order to gain an understanding of Melville's novel. Instead, by examining various analyses, they can gain numerous insights into the issues that lie under the surface of the basic plot. Studying the writings of literary critics can also aid readers in making their own assessments of *Moby-Dick* and other literary works and in developing analytical thinking skills.

The Greenhaven Literary Companion Series was created with these goals in mind. Designed for young adults, this unique anthology series provides an engaging and comprehensive introduction to literary analysis and criticism. The essays included in the Literary Companion Series are chosen for their accessibility to a young adult audience and are expertly edited in consideration of both the reading and comprehension levels of this audience. In addition, each essay is introduced by a concise summation that presents the contributing writer's main themes and insights. Every anthology in the Literary Companion Series contains a varied selection of critical essays that cover a wide time span and express diverse views. Wherever possible, primary sources are represented through excerpts from authors' notebooks, letters, and journals and through contemporary criticism.

Each title in the Literary Companion Series pays careful consideration to the historical context of the particular author or literary work. In-depth biographies and detailed chronologies reveal important aspects of authors' lives and emphasize the historical events and social milieu that influenced their writings. To facilitate further research, every anthology includes primary and secondary source bibliographies of articles and/or books selected for their suitability for young adults. These engaging features make the Greenhaven Literary Companion Series ideal for introducing students to literary analysis in the classroom or as a library resource for young adults researching the world's great authors and literature.

Exceptional in its focus on young adults, the Greenhaven Literary Companion Series strives to present literary criticism in a compelling and accessible format. Every title in the series is intended to spark readers' interest in leading American and world authors, to help them broaden their understanding of literature, and to encourage them to formulate their own analyses of the literary works that they read. It is the editors' hope that young adult readers will find these anthologies to be true companions in their study of literature.

INTRODUCTION

Decades after his death, Robert Frost remains the most quoted poet in America and one of the best-loved poets in the world. Walt Whitman and Jack Kerouac both claimed to be America's national poet, but it is Robert Frost who remains the country's quintessential poet laureate. His evocative rural scenes and simple, transfixing speech, coupled with his mastery of poetic form and meter, make his poems both memorable and pleasurable to memorize. His phrases echo in the mind long after books are shut: "Earth's the right place for love"; "I took the [road] less traveled by"; "Something there is that doesn't love a wall"; "Nothing gold can stay"; "I have promises to keep / And miles to go before I sleep." These are the words of a self-styled country poet and gentleman farmer; they are also meditations in love, religion, the nature of good and evil, and human nature.

Why study Frost? Curiosity alone should drive us. How did a man with such adversity in his life—a gambling, violent, drunkard father who left the family penniless; the deaths of several children; countless rejections before he finally "made it" at the age of forty; the grueling work of farming—come to write such profound and peaceful poetry?

According to an unlikely fan, former Soviet premier Nikita Khrushchev, Frost's poems "were full of love for the simple man." That is the key to Frost—despite his enormous talent and all of the accolades, he was first and foremost a down-to-earth man who wrote beautiful, accessible verse. And people responded with an outpouring of enthusiasm.

Frost always maintained that "the good stuff" could easily be memorized and that poetry need not be inaccessible or a chore to read. In an interview with Robert Penn Warren, Cleanth Brooks, and Kenny Withers, Frost explained why he insisted on correct meter and memorable dramatic accent and what effect he hoped his poems would produce:

Catchiness has a lot to do with it, all of it, all the way up from the ballads you hear on the street to the lines in Shakespeare that stay with you without your trying to remember them. I just say catchy. They stick on you like burrs thrown on you in holiday foolery. You don't have to remember them. It's in the way they're said, you know, an archness or something.

This "something"—the catchiness that readers take to both mind and heart—was Frost's gift. He brought musical cadence to poetry and poetry to the rhythms of everyday speech. He called this phenomenon "sound and sense," likening it to hearing a conversation in another room—even if the listener doesn't hear every word, he can understand the gist of the matter through tone of voice. The accessible tone is key. To this day, Frost remains the poet that most Americans can quote by heart; "Stopping by Woods on a Snowy Evening," "The Road Less Traveled," "Fire and Ice," "Nothing Gold Can Stay" and so many other poems have indelibly impressed not only the American canon but also the universal literary canon.

Yet Robert Frost's poems—even their titles—call for careful reading. Frost used traditional verse forms such as sonnets, dramatic monologues, and lyrics. He once said, in response to the work of free verse writers like Carl Sandburg, e.e. cummings, and even friend T.S. Eliot, that he would "as soon play tennis without a net as write free verse." He felt free verse was cheating, sloppy, and lacking in discipline. In fact, because Frost often had his speakers use colloquial speech and simple phrasing (everyday people using everyday speech), some readers are tempted to take his poems at face value and not give them (or the poet) the critical attention that they deserve. One critic admiringly said that Frost's style is so effortless that his poems are as simple and clear as someone describing the weather.

Frost is the consummate New England poet. Although the area produced many poets—Emily Dickinson, Ralph Waldo Emerson, and John Greenleaf Whittier, to name a few—it was Frost who most consistently chose the region's rural landscapes and characters to populate his poems. However, Frost's poems far transcend any physical or poetic geography, earning universal acclaim.

The essays selected for this literary companion will introduce beginning Frost readers to the poet's works. Some essays are written by poets, some by biographers, and some by literary critics. Also included are in-depth analyses of poems and the reasoning behind the poet's choices; some are prompts for independent study of a poem. Each article was selected to highlight an aspect of Frost's life or work, and will enhance the reader's understanding of a deceptively simple poet.

ROBERT FROST: A BIOGRAPHY

"He is the strongest, loneliest, friendliest poet."
—Carl Sandburg on Robert Frost

With a thick shock of prematurely white hair, squinty, piercing eyes, and a half smile on his face, Robert Frost cut a sometimes dashing, and sometimes imposing, figure. Comfortable lecturing at Ivy League schools, Frost was equally at home walking about the New England towns that he loved, stopping and discussing poetry or baseball with anyone who greeted him. He was a gentleman and a diplomat, yet he repaired his own walls, chopped his own wood, and knew the value of poultry manure in the garden. He dined with presidents and kings but so loved his students that he formed lifelong friendships with many of them. He remains the most lauded American poet of all time, at home and abroad, and his quiet poetry brought a sense of comfort to the nation through three wars, even when he himself was experiencing profound personal tragedy.

FROM SAN FRANCISCO TO NEW ENGLAND

Mention the poetry of Robert Frost to anyone—a student, teacher, or person on the street—and images of idyllic New England scenes come to mind: cobbled streets that shine in the moonlight, a sleigh ride in the winter woods, apple orchards, green meadows, handmade stone walls lining country roads, ice-laden birch trees, the glorious colors of sugar maples in autumn. These scenes are indeed important to Frost's work—it was said that he could not pass an abandoned farmhouse without wanting to "adopt" it—but Frost's life and works point to deeper, darker themes that simmer beneath the country setting. Almost four decades after his death he remains the best-known and best-loved poet of the twentieth century and a poet whose work is even more rewarding if it is studied closely.

Because he is so associated with the region, in particular

the country towns and byways of New Hampshire and Vermont, many readers are surprised to learn that Robert Frost was not born in New England. Robert Lee Frost (his father, William, though born a Northerner, was a Confederate sympathizer and named his son after the Southern general) was born on March 26, 1874, in San Francisco, California. He was artistic and dreamy even as a child; though he liked the outdoors, he equally liked the stories that his Scottish mother, Isabelle, would tell him—Celtic tales, Bible stories, and fairy tales.

When he was three years old, Frost began to hear voices and see things when left alone in a room; his father attributed this to an overactive imagination, but his mother was convinced the young Robert had inherited her gift for "second sight"—extrasensory perception. Frost was very close to his mother, both in terms of temperament and talent. He shared her love for reading and poetry and her gentle nature.

Although an imaginative child, Frost was also a typical mischievous boy. Sometimes he would skip classes, but his mother was so diligent about making sure that Robert was literate that he never fell behind in school. His father complained that she spoiled her son, but she would always say, "That Rob, he's going far."

Once, when Frost was about six years old, his father struck his mother while in a drunken rage. She moved to the East to stay with William's parents in Massachusetts, a move that would foreshadow a permanent relocation some five years later. She soon returned, however, when her in-laws sided with their son and said that she should be obedient and submissive. Most critics agree that Frost was old enough to hate his father's violent drunken streaks and that he never forgot his mother's grace in living through that hardship as a young wife and mother. Young Robert himself was whipped by his father more than once for petty infractions such as forgetting to say "please" or "excuse me." He later said that he never complained or cried out during his own beatings, but he never forgot them. The abuse of his mother bothered him more than his own whippings; when he became a father himself, he never hit his children, and he never drank liquor.

Frost's journalist father died prematurely in 1885 (although an energetic man, William Frost was a heavy drinker and inveterate gambler, addictions that contributed to his health problems). Afterwards, his mother, a poet, teacher, and deeply religious woman, moved herself, Frost, and his baby sister to Lawrence, Massachusetts, where their relatives lived. Frost hated the idea of moving in with father's parents, but the family had no choice. This move had both a moral and practical purpose: It had been William Frost's dying wish that his wife and children move to New England to be with his relatives. In addition, the family was left penniless when he died. The young widow Isabelle Frost set out cross-country with young Robert and his sister, Jeanie, with only eight dollars to see them through.

Lawrence, Massachusetts, a blue-collar city near the New Hampshire border, was the home of Frost's paternal grandparents and would be his home through his adolescence. Frost had trouble adjusting to life in New England. Although he excelled in high school, he sometimes got into fights because of his cutting wit. Frost's grandparents resented his mother: Unable to accept their late son's addictions, they blamed Isabelle for his death. Their coldness extended to Robert, and they rarely showed him any affection or encouragement. Thus, Frost, his mother, and his sister lived at poverty level for some time. To compound his feelings of isolation, Frost also found himself among students with no artistic ambitions and who rarely attended school past sixth grade: children usually went to work in mills or on farms. It was during his first two years of high school that Frost began to write poetry. The solitary nature of the activity suited him and helped ease the loneliness he felt as a teenager. His first poem, published by the Lawrence High newspaper during his sophomore year, was about Hernán Cortés.

COURTSHIP AND MARRIAGE, PARENTHOOD AND ADULTHOOD

Frost could find no kindred spirits in New England until he met a girl during his senior year of high school—Elinor White—who shared his love of poetry and matched him intellectually. Her approval meant much to him; when he had a volume of five of his early poems printed just for her and she reacted unenthusiastically, he left for the Carolinas and the great dismal swamp in a fit of dejection. Frost thought this trip would be a way to make her feel guilty about not appreciating his love for her. The adventure lasted only a few days. He wired his mother that he was coming home and returned penniless and in poor health. Elinor, impressed by the dramatic, albeit foolish, gesture, took him back.

Upon graduating at the top of his class (his covaledictorian at Lawrence High was Elinor), he pursued higher education but left college twice: the first time, he dropped out of Dartmouth College. Dartmouth was the college that his paternal grandparents ordered him to attend. Since they were funding his education, they felt they were entitled to control where and how he studied. Frost resented their meddling, and despite his attempts to fit in, he was miserable at Dartmouth. He joined a fraternity there, but instead of drinking with the brothers, he would disappear for walks in the New Hampshire woods. Missing his mother and Elinor, he left after seven weeks. He went to work in a wool mill hoping to save enough money to get married. It was horrible, backbreaking work. This experience, coupled with his later experiences as a farmer, would give Frost a deep respect for all blue-collar workers, a respect that was evident in many of his poems.

When Frost turned twenty-one, Elinor agreed to marry him. They married in December 1895, and the following spring Elinor realized that she was pregnant. She gave birth to their first child, a boy named Elliott. He was, by all accounts, a sweet-tempered, beautiful child. Frost felt confident that he could now build the family life that he lacked as a child.

Revitalized, Frost decided to give college another try, this time at Harvard University. His essays in his letters of application and his high school grades were impressive enough to merit him entrance. Frost enrolled in Harvard in hopes of studying under the tutelage of William James (the famous psychologist and brother of Henry James, the novelist). Ironically, William James was on sabbatical during the semester that Frost matriculated at Harvard. The absence of a potential mentor, and his disappointment with the program, caused Frost to again drop out. Some friends speculated that he was too "down-to-earth" for the academic types that he encountered there. Additionally, while there, he often commuted to Lawrence to help his mother, who was in failing health, teach in her school. The schedule taxed him physically, and he became ill. To compound matters, Elinor had become pregnant again. So, for a combination of reasons, Frost permanently abandoned his studies shortly thereafter. Lesley, the Frosts' second child, was born the month after he left Harvard. As he moved away from student life, his family took on more importance.

Three-year-old Elliott became ill suddenly. Elinor's mother was visiting at the time and thought that Elliott's sickness was just an intestinal flu. She advised Elinor to concentrate on baby Lesley and told her that, as a Christian Scientist, she would pray for Elliott's quick recovery. Frost was not so trusting. He called a doctor, who arrived the next day. The doctor, after berating Elinor and Frost for not calling him sooner, informed the young parents that their son had only hours to live: He was suffering from an advanced case of cholera. Elliott died that night.

After Elliott's death, Frost felt that the family needed to move. Their house was tainted by sadness and death. Frost's paternal grandparents bought him the Derry farm in New Hampshire in 1899. Frost suspected that, rather than being a goodwill gesture, his grandparents wanted to get rid of him and see him fail; however, the city boy adapted surprisingly well to rural life. It was a tumultuous time. Frost dealt with his grief over Elliott's death by burying himself in his work—farming and writing. One of the poems from this time is "Home Burial." He delighted in watching Lesley grow, but he again felt sadness when his mother died of cancer within six months of Elliott.

Frost would live on the Derry farm for ten years, until 1909, and have four more children during the time there—Carol, Irma, Marjorie, and Elinor, who would die in infancy. In the wake of the deaths of his mother, Elliott, and young Elinor, Frost realized that life was precious and tried to make life sweet for his surviving children. He would let them stay up late on warm summer evenings to look at the stars and would make them wooden animal menageries. Frost taught his children to identify tiny plants, insects and flowers, to examine snow crystals as they fell on the dark fabric of their coats, to identify the stars and constellations, to recognize an animal by its call, and to be aware of the cycle of life, death, and rebirth in nature. Occasionally he would read them stories about King Arthur and perform the dramatic voices for them. He was lavish with book allowances for them, but he insisted that they not read "junk" like comic books. His favorite books were the Bible, works by Edgar Allan Poe, James Fenimore Cooper, Ivan Turgenev, Willa Cather, Ernest Hemingway, Horace, Virgil, Shakespeare, John Milton, John Keats, William Wordsworth, Percy Shelley, Lord Byron, Matthew Arnold, Thomas Hardy, and

William James. He often said that Rudyard Kipling's *The Jungle Book* was an absolute favorite since he could read it to his children and watch them delight in it, too. "I would read it to any child who asked," he said.

Slowly, life seemed to return to normal. Although financial circumstances did not demand that he rely solely on farming as a way of life—he would write poetry late at night after finishing chores—Frost certainly learned enough about both the idylls and the dark side of country life to earn his reputation as a rustic figure. He would carry a notebook with him when he went to milk his cows at midnight: (He milked them at that time since at four in the morning, the conventional milking hour, he would often be writing at the kitchen table or fast asleep there). Though the life was hard, it was valuable to Frost: No bit of natural life or change in the landscape was too trivial to escape Frost's scrutiny. So taken was he by the land that he felt he needed to write about it. One of his favorite sayings was that the scythe and the pen were his favorite tools. But farming alone was not enough for him.

In 1906 he began teaching at Pinkerton Academy in Derry. Though he never finished college, the Pinkerton faculty was happy to make an exception for the talented young man (even the dean of Harvard University was impressed with his intellect and his natural ability with language). Frost was an exciting teacher who would ask students philosophical questions and get to know them well. When analyzing his teaching style, many critics drew parallels between Frost the teacher and Frost the poet. His laid-back temperament and his love of the quiet, philosophical nature of authors such as William James and Ralph Waldo Emerson were reflected in his classroom. In fact, at the beginning of his career, Frost taught psychology, not writing. He would teach many other subjects as well, including Latin and history. His students in both the psychology and writing classes often spoke about Frost's unconventional methods. He would cancel class if the weather was too nice. He sometimes had the students sit with their backs to him and memorize lessons (an Oriental method that apparently worked well). He would ignore lazy students and concentrate on and befriend those who showed enthusiasm for the subject. He required virtually no tests or exams, and he thought students should revel in a subject rather than be drilled in it. "Don't write unless you have something to say. If you don't have it, get it!" he would say.

He would teach at Pinkerton until 1910 and then at a teachers college in Plymouth, New Hampshire, until 1912.

A CHANGE OF SCENERY

In 1912, despite the support of his wife and children, his lack of success as a poet began to affect Frost physically and emotionally. He wanted to see his work in print, and he wanted to make his living on poetry alone, farming or teaching for pleasure, not out of necessity. Manuscripts containing poems that would later garner him Pulitzers piled up on the kitchen table, rejected by publishers in New England and New York. Elinor and he shared a passionate, sometimes emotionally draining marriage. Elinor withdrew into herself after the deaths of Elliott and Elinor, and though she fought her depression, Frost felt that she had a hard time opening up to him beyond small talk. He felt constrained and frustrated. Farmhouse living, although idyllic, was also isolating, and they had very little contact with other couples. They also began to argue about how to raise the children. Frost developed chest pains and was deeply depressed. In 1912, in a last-ditch effort to save himself and what he felt was his vocation, Frost used a small annual pension and took the family to England. Elinor was thrilled; she had always wanted to live in England. An amateur botanist who loved to explore the forests and meadows of New England, Frost delighted in roaming the British countryside and seeing new flora. Most importantly, while there he met the leading British poets of the day: Edward Thomas, Ezra Pound, T.S. Eliot, and William Butler Yeats. He maintained lifelong friendships and acquaintances with these men—even friendly rivalries. He liked to argue with T.S. Eliot about Scottish poets like Robert Burns. Eliot considered Burns a balladeer. Frost, proud of his Scottish heritage and a lover of Burns's work, thought Eliot was stuck-up. These meetings with colleagues helped Frost raise his poetry to a higher level. Ironically, it was in England that he was able to find a publisher for his first book of poems, *A Boy's Will* (1913), a book laden with New England images. Ezra Pound loved the book and used his enormous influence to write to American publishers about this "fine young poet." The letters worked; in 1914 Frost's second, groundbreaking book of poems, *North of Boston*, was published in America. The book was a great success, quickly selling thousands of copies in both America and England. At the time, however, there was unrest in England. Archduke Francis Ferdinand was assassinated in 1914, and by the summer of that year Europe was at war. Frost felt they needed to return to the United States, that it would be unpatriotic to stay. He, Elinor, and their four children returned to America in February 1915. The man who left America as a chicken farmer returned a celebrity. Literary magazines knew his name, and suddenly the schools and academic cliques that had rejected Frost were courting him. He became a teacher at many New England colleges: Harvard, Amherst, Dartmouth, and Middlebury, founding the Bread Loaf School of English at Middlebury in Vermont. By the time *Mountain Interval* was published in 1916, Frost was already on the lecture circuit, traveling to colleges all across North America.

LATER ADULTHOOD: TRIALS AND TRIUMPHS

Except for these three years spent with his wife and children in London (1912–1915), Frost remained a poet-farmer in New Hampshire and Vermont, for most of his adult life, and it was these two states with which he most identified himself and his poetry. The volume of poetry entitled *New Hampshire* won Frost his first Pulitzer Prize in 1924. Frost had come into his own as a poet, and the book was a tour de force, containing poems such as "Fire and Ice," "Stopping by Woods on a Snowy Evening," and "The Axe-Helve." This was just the start of a later adulthood that saw rich successes after his relatively late publication (Frost was forty when *A Boy's Will* was printed). After the relatively light sales of *West-Running Brook*, Frost vowed that he would "take his own advice and write only important stuff" when inspired—never for publishers' deadlines.

For Frost, the 1930s were reminiscent of the Derry farm days: sweet times tempered by tragedy. In 1930 he published his *Collected Poems*, and critics acknowledged that Frost was part of the poetic canon, standing alongside poets like Shakespeare and Wordsworth as "required reading"; both *Collected Poems* and *A Further Range* (1936) would garner him Pulitzers. Frost's work, simple and appealing to everyone from factory workers to literary critics, set him apart from poets such as T.S. Eliot, whose cryptic poetry was hard to understand. In the aftermath of the Great Depression, Frost's plain-spoken poems about rural folk were welcome.

On subway newsstands, magazines featuring Frost sold as well as those featuring celebrities from film and stage. Yet the thirties also gave Frost three blows to his personal life. In 1934 Frost's sickly daughter Marjorie died from consumption after giving birth to a child. It was a blow to the family, but since Marjorie had always been ill, they looked upon her death as a mixed blessing.

The second shock came in 1938. Frost, Elinor, and son Carol were vacationing in Florida when Elinor suffered a massive, fatal heart attack. Frost was devastated. He collapsed, unable to eat, sleep, or even think correctly for months afterwards. He told a friend that Elinor was "the unspoken half of everything I ever wrote." He continued on the lecture circuit in an attempt to immerse himself in his work, but recovery was slow. Frost was revived somewhat by an unconventional relationship with his social secretary, Kathleen Morrison, who became his girl Friday after Elinor's death in 1938. Morrison was the wife of one of Frost's colleagues from the Bread Loaf School of English. It was clear to Frost's friends that he had become infatuated with Morrison, who was many years younger than he. Although the two never became romantically involved, Morrison remained Frost's secretary, public relations person, close friend, and caretaker until his death. Her youthful presence and kindness revitalized him, but the memories of Elinor, his great love, haunted him until his death.

A third, equally unseen tragedy occurred in 1940. His son, Carol, had always suffered from depression—Frost suspected, after viewing his father's own violently erratic behavior during his childhood, that mental illness ran in the family. Frost tried to counsel Carol, thinking that grief over his mother's death was weighing heavily on the young man. Carol was resentful of his father's success, however, and although Frost supported his children heartily, it would never be enough for Carol. He wanted to make a name for himself as a writer, but he lacked his father's talent and patience. Feeling bitter and hopeless about achieving fame as a poet, he shot himself, dying less than two years after his mother.

Frost slowly but surely emerged from personal darkness during the 1940s. When *A Witness Tree* won the Pulitzer in 1943, Frost became the first four-time Pulitzer winner in America. He lectured at Harvard and Dartmouth; ironically, the two colleges from which he withdrew as a young man.

Yet he felt vaguely ill at ease at both campuses. Harvard felt snobby to him, and Dartmouth seemed too distant. College think tanks were engrossed with World War II and had no time for poets, Frost thought. Frost was certainly sympathetic to the Allied cause—his book *Steeple Bush* (1947) talks about the effects of war—but he felt that wartime was the time to honor poetry's sustaining power rather than brush it aside. He refused to join other poets who wrote political commentary into their works, such as Carl Sandburg.

Ironically, it was in "apolitical" Frost that the nation took refuge, and his fame rose during the turmoil of World War II. Shortly after the end of the war, *Complete Poems* was published, going straight to the top of the best-seller lists. Frost gave comfort to Americans through his quiet, strong, neighborly persona. Even as he published more experimental works like the drama *A Masque of Reason*, he never lost touch with the common man. He once commented that one of the jobs that gave him the most delight was lecturing to young people; during the forties, he lectured to soldiers in training while at Dartmouth.

Frost's triumphs lasted into the 1950s; and these triumphs lasted because *Frost* lasted. He was spry and energetic, even in his eighties. Congress honored him repeatedly, and each honor seemed to revitalize him, particularly his post as honorary consultant in the humanities at the Library of Congress. Even during the restructuring of the fifties and the revolutionary sixties, Frost remained the dean of American poets, popular with both critics and the general public.

The golden boys of the century were gone—T.S. Eliot, William Faulkner, Ernest Hemingway, and F. Scott Fitzgerald had all died or fallen by the wayside in terms of talent. But Frost was still writing, still lecturing, and still relevant. Even Oxford and Cambridge broke tradition and honored a "Yank" in 1957, bestowing honorary degrees on Frost and recognizing him not only as an American icon but also as a universal poet.

In the late 1950s and early 1960s, Frost became friends with upcoming poets Wallace Stevens, Robert Lowell, John Crowe Ransom, and W.H. Auden. Frost is best known, however, for his special relationship with John F. Kennedy. He liked the young Democrat from Massachusetts because he was "literate" and valued poetry and the arts as much as science and space travel. In fact, Frost predicted Kennedy's win at a Christmas party prior to the election year. Kennedy, who had loved Frost's work since boyhood, quoted Frost often during speeches, especially "Death of the Hired Man" and "Stopping by Woods on a Snowy Evening". He often closed conferences by saying, "I have promises to keep, and miles to go before I sleep." In November 1960 Kennedy asked Frost to compose a poem and read it at his January inauguration. It was the first time that an artist had been recognized in such a political event.

The morning of Kennedy's inauguration was bitterly cold and windy, despite the brilliant winter sunlight. Frost had failing eyesight, and his already poor eyes were irritated by the wind and the sun's glare. He found himself blinded as he rose to read. Instead of panicking or bowing out, however, Frost recited a poem from memory, "The Gift Outright," which was about the debt owed to America and to the earth itself. The recitation was dramatic and perfect. As the white-haired gentleman farmer-poet from New Hampshire stood before the young president it seemed as if bridges were built through that one symbolic gesture showing that the young and the old, the politician and the poet, could work together.

But that was not Frost's last public recitation. Nikita Khrushchev, the much feared leader of the Soviet Union, liked Frost immensely and hosted him in Russia in 1962. Yet Frost, who never made public displays of emotion, let his feelings about belligerent Russian actions be known. At one dinner in Moscow, he recited his poem "Mending Wall." "Something there is that doesn't love a wall, / That sets the frozen-ground-swell under it. . . . Before I built a wall I'd ask to know / What I was walling in or walling out, / And to whom I was like to give offense." Western Europe and America in particular knew that Frost was reprimanding the erection of the Berlin Wall and applauded the gentle, effective way that the poet made his point.

The trips, his schedule, and his age took their toll. Frost was in failing health when he returned to New England. He survived cancer, prostate problems, and gastrointestinal illness only to be felled by a pulmonary embolism. He still read and wrote while in the hospital; in fact, it was announced that his last book, *In the Clearing*, had won the 1962 Bollingen Prize. His resilience and vitality astounded people, and his strong hands and sturdy frame stayed with him into his later years: Everyone expected the octogenarian to pull through. Thus, the nation was shocked when Frost's death was announced on January 29, 1963. In Brigham Hospital in Boston, he complained of chest pains and shortness of breath, went into shock, and died quickly. He was almost eighty-nine years old. Condolences poured in from every corner of the globe. Schoolchildren in Frost's old hometown of Lawrence, Massachusetts, wrote letters filled with grief at his passing.

Since his death, many poets publicly acknowledged their debt to Frost or emulated him in their own works—particularly W.H. Auden, Elizabeth Bishop, and Seamus Heaney. Frost's work has been translated into every major modern language and, as a sign of esteem, an annual festival in his adopted hometown of Lawrence, Massachusetts, celebrates his life and work. Over one hundred years after his birth, Frost's legacy lives and thrives.

CHAPTER 1

Robert Frost: His Work and Life

Poetry as Extravagance

Robert Frost

In this lecture or "talk," as Frost preferred to call his public speaking engagements, the poet tries to explain to a young audience the purpose of poetry and why it counts. In the end, he says, it is a necessary luxury—an extravagance.

I think the first thing I ought to speak of is all this luxuriance: all in easy chairs and a beautiful hall—and nothing to do but to listen to me. Pretty soft, I call it. Pretty soft.

I was so made that I—though a Vermonter and all that—I never took any stock in the doctrine that "a penny saved is a penny earned." A penny saved is a mean thing, and a penny spent, you know, is a generous thing and a big thing—like this, you see. It took more than a penny to do this. There's nothing mean about it.

And one of the expressions I like best is—in the Bible it is and in poets—they say, "of no mean city am I." That's a great saying, ain't it?—to be "of no mean city," like San Francisco, Boston. People deprecate our beautiful cities, and I go around thinking how many people living in them must say that—"of no mean city am I," you know. How splendid. And "of no mean college am I." (Funny for me to be talking about that.)

And I was thinking—I am going to read to you, of course, principally—I was thinking of the extravagance of the universe, you know, what an *extravagant* universe it is. And the most extravagant thing in it, as far as we know, is man—the most wasteful, spending thing in it—in all his luxuriance, you know. And how stirring it is, the sun and everything. Take a telescope and look as far as you will, you know. How much of a universe was wasted just to produce puny us. It's wonderful, it fills you with awe.

And poetry is a sort of extravagance, in many ways. It's something that people wonder about. What's the need of it?—

Excerpted from Robert Frost, "On Extravagance: A Talk," in *Frost: Collected Poems* (Library of America edition). Reprinted by permission of the Estate of Robert Frost.

you know. And the answer is, no need—not particularly. That is, that's the first one.

DOES POETRY MATTER?

I've always enjoyed being around colleges, nominally as a professor, you know, and a puzzle to everybody as to what I was doing—whether any thing or not, you know. (You'd like to leave that to others. Never would defend myself there.) And people say to me occasionally, "Where *does* poetry come in?" Some of you may be thinking it tonight: "What's it all for? Does it *count?*"

POETRY AND WOMEN

When I catch a man reading my book, red-handed, you know, he usually looks up cheerfully and says, "My wife is a great fan of yours." Puts it off on the women. And I figured that out lately—that there's an indulgence of poetry, a manly indulgence of poetry, that's a good deal like the manly indulgence of women, see. You know, we say that women rule the world. That's a nice way to talk. And we say that poetry rules the world. There's a poem that says:

> We are the music-makers,
>   And we are the dreamers of dreams, . . .
> World-losers and world-forsakers,

and all that. We are "the makers" of the future. We

> Built Nineveh with our sighing,
>   And Babel itself with our mirth;
> And o'erthrew them with prophesying
>   To the old of the new world's worth;

—you see—

> For each age is a dream that is dying,
>   And one that is coming to birth.

That's a big claim, isn't it? An exaggerated claim.

But I look on the universe as a kind of an exaggeration anyway, the whole business, see. That's the way you think of it: great, great, great expense—everybody trying to make it mean something more than it is.

But all poetry asks is to be accorded the same indulgence that women are accorded. And I think the women, the ladies, are perhaps the go-betweens, you know. They're our ambassadors to the men. They break the poetry to the men. And it's a strange thing that men write the poetry more than the women; that is, the world's history is full of men poets and very few women. Women are in the dative case. It's to and for them—the poetry. And then for men and the affairs of men through them. (One knows the story that makes an argument that women really run the world in the end, you know, run everything.)

And I'm not defending at all. I just thought one of the figures of poetry—it's a metaphor, isn't it? you know, various kinds of metaphor—but one of the figures you never hear mentioned is just the one extravagance. See. This is a little extravaganza, this little poem. And to what extent is it excessive? And can you go with it? Some people can't. And sometimes it's a bitter extravagance, like that passage in Shakespeare that so many make their novels out of: life is a tale told by an idiot, signifying nothing, you know. That's an extravagance, of course—of bitterness.

POETRY IS NOT PREACHING

And people hold you. You say something sad or something pessimistic and something cynical, and they forget to allow for the extravagance of poetry—that you're not saying that all the time. That's not a doctrine you're preaching. You loathe anybody that wants you to be either pessimist or optimist. It doesn't belong to it; it doesn't belong at all. Are you happy or are you unhappy? Why are you? You know, you have no right to ask.

The extravagance lies in "it sometimes seems as if." See. That would be a good name of a book: "it sometimes seems as if." Or it says: "if only you knew." You could put that on the cover of a book. "If only I could tell you," you know. "Beyond participation lie my sorrows and beyond relief," you know; and yet you're harping on them, you see, in that way.

I arrived step by step at these things about it all, myself. I've been thinking lately that politics is an extravagance, again, an extravagance about *grievances.* And poetry is an extravagance about *grief.* And grievances are something that can be remedied, and griefs are irremediable, you know. And there you take them with a sort of a happy sadness. You know that they say drink helps—say it does. "Make you happy," the song goes, you know, the college song goes, "Make you happy, make you sad . . . sad. . . ." That old thing. How deep those things go.

So I suppose that leads me to say an extravagance. I think I have right here one. Let's see it. It's made out in larger print

for me by my publishers. And I remember somebody holding it up for some doctrine that's supposed to be in it, you
know. It begins with this kind of a person:

> He thought he kept the universe alone;

See, just that one line could be a whole poem, you know.

> He thought he kept the universe alone;

That's the way he felt that day.

> For all the voice in answer he could wake
> Was but the mocking echo of his own
> From some tree-hidden cliff across the lake.
> Some morning from the boulder-broken beach
> He would cry out on life, that what it wants
> Is not its own love back in copy speech,
> But counter-love, original response.

See, that's what's one of the terrible things that's lacking, see.

> Is not its own love back in copy speech,
> But counter-love, original response.
> And nothing ever came of what he cried
> Unless it was the embodiment that crashed
> In the cliff's talus on the other side,
> And then in the far distant water splashed,
> But after a time allowed for it to swim,
> Instead of proving human when it neared
> And someone else additional to him,
> As a great buck it powerfully appeared,
> Pushing the crumpled water up ahead,
> And landed pouring like a waterfall,
> And stumbled through the rocks with horny tread,
> And forced the underbrush—and that was all.

That's all he got out of his longing, you see. (And somebody
made quite an attack on that as not satisfying the noblest in
our nature or something, you know.) He missed it all. All he
got was this beautiful thing, didn't he? And then:

> Unless it was the embodiment that crashed
> In the cliff's talus on the other side,
> And then in the far distant water splashed,
> But after a time allowed for it to swim,
> Instead of proving human when it neared

This person expected it to be, I think.

> Instead of proving human when it neared
> And someone else additional to him,
> As a great buck it powerfully appeared,
> Pushing the crumpled water

And he didn't get anything out of that, you know.

> And forced the underbrush—and that was all.

But that's just by way of carrying it over from what I was talking. I usually, you know, talk without any reference to my own poems—talk politics or something.

And then, just thinking of extravagances, back through the years—this is one, with a title like this: "Never Again Would Birds' Song Be the Same." You see, this is another tone of extravagance:

He would declare and could himself believe

See, this is beginning to be an extravagance right in that line, isn't it?

He would declare

—you know, defiantly—

                    and could himself believe
That the birds there in all the garden round
From having heard the daylong voice of Eve
Had added to their own an oversound,
Her tone of meaning though without the words.
Admittedly an eloquence so soft
Could only have had an influence on birds
When call or laughter carried it aloft.
Be that as may be, she was in their song.
Moreover her voice upon their voices crossed
Had now persisted in the woods so long
That probably it never would be lost.
Never again would birds' song be the same.
And to do that to birds was why she came.

See. They used to write extravagant things to ladies' eyebrows, you know. See, that's part—one of the parts of poetry.

And now I can see some people are incapable of taking it, that's all. And I'm not picking you out. I do this on a percentage basis. And I can tell by expression of faces how troubled they are, just about that. I think it's the extravagance of it that's bothering them. . . .

And my extravagance would go on from there to say that people think that life is a *result* of certain atoms coming together, see, instead of being the *cause* that brings the atoms together. See, there's something to be said about that in the utter, utter extravagant way. . . .

I like to see you. I like to bother some of you. What do we go round with poetry for? Go round just for kindred spirits some way—not for criticism, not for appreciation, and nothing but just awareness of each other about it all. . . .

Then go back to just in general—see if I've got anything else there. No. Yeah. This is slippery. No, I'll just say them, I guess—little ones now. Some old ones I'll mix with some

new ones. The first poem I ever read in public, in 1915, was
at Tufts College, and this was it—1915:

Two roads diverged in a yellow wood,
And sorry I could not travel both
And be one traveler, long I stood
And looked down one as far as I could
To where it bent in the undergrowth;

Then took the other, as just as fair,
And having perhaps the better claim,
Because it was grassy and wanted wear;
Though as for that the passing there
Had worn them really about the same,

And both that morning equally lay
In leaves no step had trodden black.
Oh, I kept the first for another day!
Yet knowing how way leads on to way,
I doubted if I should ever come back.

I shall be telling this with a sigh
Somewhere ages and ages hence:
Two roads diverged in a wood, and I—
I took the one less traveled by,
And that has made all the difference.

Then—that's an old one—then another old one, quite a
different tone. You see, this one is more casual talking, this
next one:

Whose woods these are I think I know.
His house is in the village though;
He will not see me stopping here
To watch his woods fill up with snow.

My little horse must think it queer
To stop without a farmhouse near
Between the woods and frozen lake
The darkest evening of the year.

He gives his harness bells a shake
To ask if there is some mistake.
The only other sound's the sweep
Of easy wind and downy flake.

The woods are lovely, dark and deep,
But I have promises to keep,
And miles to go before I sleep,
And miles to go before I sleep.

And that—I won't use the word extravagance again this
evening. I swear off. You know sometimes a talk is just trying to run away from one word. If you get started using it you
can't get away from it, sometimes.

The Quietly Overwhelming Robert Frost

Milton Bracker

In an interview from 1958, poet and *New York Times* special correspondent Milton Bracker examines the enormous popularity of Robert Frost, a popularity usually only associated with star athletes or celebrities. Bracker notes that, in person, Frost seems exactly like the persona of so many of his poems: rustic, energetic, serious, and witty. In this interview, Frost talks about many subjects related to poetry, including its accessibility to the average reader and his own popularity.

Robert Frost is a poet whose work and personal appearances have moved thousands of Americans to a demonstrativeness that might easily be associated with the presence of a heroic athlete or a movie star. When he says his poems (the verb he insists on—he never "reads" them), it is to standing-room-only audiences. And the response is based not on superficial idolatry but on a deep-set and affectionate admiration often bordering on awe.

At 84, Robert Frost has won four Pulitzer Prizes and been cited by more institutions of higher learning than there are in any college football conference. He has jested that he would rather get a degree than an education; but this is simply to be gracious to the donors. Actually, he has not only had an education of his own (though never a baccalaureate degree) but as a teacher, both fixed and itinerant, has contributed preferred shares of stock to the educational portfolios held by several generations of scholars.

But the impact of Robert Frost on poetry and on those who love it is possibly less than his impact as a personality on anyone who gets near him. If you have had considerable experience in "interviewing" people, you are still not prepared for this white-haired New Englander (who, improbably, was born in San Francisco) because he is like no statesman, celebrity or ordinary human being you have ever interviewed. Robert Frost, newly honored by appointment as poetry consultant to the Library of Congress, is quietly but unmistakably overwhelming.

"There's nothing in me to be afraid of," he will assure you. "I'm too offhand; I'm an offhander." But there is a deadly joke in his offhandedness. As he says, slipping it in casually, in another connection, "I bear watching." Moreover, he will let you know disarmingly that "I'm not confused; I'm only well-mixed." And he might have added of himself, as he frequently remarks of certain of his most-quoted and picked-apart poems, that he is "loaded with ulteriority."

"You have to look out for everybody's metaphors," says Robert Frost. He himself is perhaps the biggest metaphor of all. He even *looks* like a symbol. His hair is really white and really silky; a mass of it tends to sift down to the left side of his forehead like snow to one corner of a window. His eyes are pale blue, cragged by heavy brows with white curls wintering them. His lower lip is the thicker; it juts a little. In the over-all he is massive, often understandably likened to roughhewn granite. He had an "altercation with a surgeon"—there is a virtually imperceptible scar on his right cheek. But the real scar is the scar of living, and no man ever wore it more proudly or with more stunning effect, as photographers have discovered.

Even in the impersonal formality of a New York hotel room, he would prefer to be tieless. He wears high black shoes, and is apt to leave them half unlaced. His hands show virtually no spots of age. His grip is firm and wholly unself-conscious. And when he walks down an aisle to a stage or platform, he strides strongly and directly, as completely in command of the situation as of the loyalty and awe of those in the audience. His voice is resonant to the level of being gravelly; he may use it to repeat things he has said many times before. But he is psychologically incapable of speaking a cliché, or of arranging words in a commonplace manner.

Still, an interview has to have a "plan of campaign," Robert Frost acknowledged. So what more natural than a little starter about his new job? He seized upon the word "consultant" in his new title. "As the greatest living authority on education," he began, with a twinkle, "I particularly want to be consulted by the foundations."

Robert Frost has had one publisher for forty-three years. His books have sold more than 400,000 copies and he has actually made a living out of poetry, although he once had to give up buying a painting he wanted because he could not get it for $1,000. But the implication was clear: If, through his new post, he could interest those who might assist other poets, he was eager to do so. . . .

"You can't make a poem without a point." He laughed, remembering having said it another way: "You've got to snap the quip to make Pegasus prance." Robert Frost is much too human not be pleased by his own phrase-making. "Snap the quip," he repeated, with a chuckle. "I could make up a joke at a banquet, use it in a different way at another banquet. I'm very instructive; I'm very accidental. I go barding around, and all that. Barding around."

He frequently "bards around" with college presidents and has warm regard and great respect for several. "But I'm aware that some of them have no interest in it, and that's all right," he said. Again the raised brows, the fleeting laugh that lights up the weathered face like a sudden shaft of sunlight. "They *have* to be present when they decorate me," he added. Then, more seriously, "I'm not as anxious about poetry as I am about these poor college presidents." Apart from the problems faced by the educators, there was a criterion he liked to apply: "He's on our side." He mentioned four of whom that might be said, then fretted a little lest he had left out some others. He is always elliptical in his language; never in his sense of friendship.

Robert Frost has defined poetry as "that which is lost from prose and verse in translation." As for the great poets, Shakespeare "knew more about psychiatry and people like Othello and Desdemona" than any $25-an-hour man. Robert Frost considered the Moor for a moment as an analyst's patient. "The psychiatrist would advise him not to smother her," he decided. Then his quick eyes changed reflectively. "But some of them are awful good at it," he admitted.

He was reminded of his own insights—his incredible exactness with words, as when, in "Blue-Butterfly Day," he wrote of the wheels that "freshly sliced the April mire," thus choosing the absolutely correct verb, the one so uniquely evocative as to renew and fix for many readers the experience of observing such a wheel in such mud for all time. And the other exactnesses: the swimming buck pushing the *crumpled* water; the ice crystals from the birch branch *avalanching* on the snow crust.

Robert Frost's browned face crinkled at the references. "That's what I live for," he said—the appreciation, in detail, of the essential purity of his work. "It cuts a little edge across your feelings," he said. Then he talked of the American attitude toward poetry, of the time he and a distinguished scientist met and he had begun, "Let's you and I compare science and poetry, that's what I live for." The other said, "You mean the exactness of science and the inexactness of poetry." "'Oh,' I said," said Robert Frost, "'you mean poetry is inexact. If you mean that, I'm going home.' He said 'Let's change the subject.'"

"IT AIN'T TENNIS"
In this excerpt, Frost biographer Jeffrey Meyers highlights this famous quote in which Frost stresses the need for discipline in poetry during a repartee with fellow poet Carl Sandburg.

In one of his famous comparisons, directed mainly against his popular rival Carl Sandburg, Frost refused to abandon the rules of poetry and said he would as soon write free verse as play tennis with the net down. When Sandburg took up the challenge and insisted that "you can play a better game with the net down," Frost triumphantly replied: "Sure you can play a better game with the net down—and without the racket and balls—but it ain't tennis."

Jeffrey Meyers, *Robert Frost: A Biography*, New York: Houghton Mifflin, 1996, pp. 80–81.

And he told of the diplomat who had spent a lot on modern art, and liked to be regarded as something of an expert on it, but who remarked of a young relative with poetic inclinations, "We hoped he'd get over it." Robert Frost had not enjoyed that. On the other hand, he knew businessmen who really had "this same gentle weakness for the arts."

"A man will say, 'I'm just an engineer,'" he went on, "yet he will read more poetry than anyone I know."

And he linked this to the "greatest triumph in life: that's

what everything turns on. To be reminded of something you hardly knew you knew." He said it gave you the feeling, "Oh what a good boy am I."

Then, inevitably, I brought up "Stopping by Woods on a Snowy Evening." He had "said" this a few nights before at the New School, pronouncing it a little rapidly, a little too rapidly to permit the emotion of those in the audience (who had been gripped by it for anywhere from thirty minutes to thirty years) to break out in applause. There is of course a growing literature about these sixteen lines; and Robert Frost took it in stride. "Now, that's all right," he said, "it's out of my hands once it's published." His protagonist might have said

> *But I have promises to keep,*
> *And miles to go before I sleep,*

simply because he was having a pleasant social evening, and it was time to go home. Yet Robert Frost knew it had often been taken as a "death poem."

"I never intended that," he said, "but I did have the feeling it was loaded with ulteriority." He said it was written one night back in the Twenties, when he was a "little excited from getting overtired, they call it overintoxicated." In the second stanza he made what he has called an "unnecessary commitment"—the line

> *My little horse must think it queer*

But he rode it out: he "triumphed over it." And, he went on, there was "that thing about every poem. I didn't see the end until I got to it. Every poem is a voyage of discovery. I go in to see if I can get out, like you go to the North Pole. Once you've said the first line, the rest of it's got to be."

Robert Frost leaned heavily toward his visitor as, on a rostrum, he seems to move gradually closer to each individual in the hall.

"The glory of any particular poem," he continued, "is once you've tasted that arrival at the end. That's what makes all the difference." But in poetry, as in other struggles, the defeats need not be "inglorious." Again, as always, with Robert Frost, it was doing what had to be done and doing it bravely. It was the triumph of spirit over matter. It was people "not believing, and then having to believe."

Robert Frost has one "ruthless purpose" and that is poetry. But he is as aware of the police story on page one of the morning paper as of the so-called advent of the space age. He takes it all in perspective. He was at Kitty Hawk in 1893, before the Wright Brothers. Some time after their historic flight, he wrote a poem called "Kitty Hawk." Thus early aeronautics and recent rocketry are in a sense the same to him; they are both part of the "great enterprise of the spirit into matter." Science is the great "lock-picker." Science goes "on, on, on, but the wonder of philosophy is that it stops." Since man knew all along that the moon and the planets were there, it was inevitable that scientists would be "risking spirit" to get there. And that poets would write of where they were trying to get, and why.

As for Robert Frost himself:

"About one-tenth of my poems are astronomical; and I've had a glass a good deal of the time." He meant a telescope but, as in so many things he says, the figurative interpretation was at least as accurate. He said the young missile men were doing a "fine, daring, bold thing." They were sharing the "great event of history"—science—and science meant the "dash of the spirit into the material," no matter how remote. . . .

The conversation narrowed back to Robert Frost himself. He spoke of sleep, "Just as I feel I never have to go to sleep," he said, "little dreams begin to come over me, voices, sometimes, and I know I am gone. There is a curious connection between reverie, meditation and dreams." The very night before, he had dreamed of stumbling and falling. And often, he would dream of a boyhood experience when, mistaken in thinking "I bore a charmed life," he got a "terrible dose of hornets." Now he dreams of the hornets, yet never so deeply as to be unaware of his actual situation. "I'm aware of the blankets," he said, a little wonderingly. Safe in bed, he pulls them up over his head and thwarts the dream-swarm.

He said a magazine had recently listed him as "one of the oldest living men."

"Funny, isn't it, about living on," he mused. "They didn't educate me when I was young—the doctor said I was delicate and wouldn't live long. That's probably what prolongs life."

He went further into paradox.

"I'm not the kind of man who thinks the world can be saved by knowledge. It can only be saved by daring, bravery, going ahead. . . . I have done many things that it looked as if it was impossible to do—like going on the platform. I did it because I didn't have to face bullets." He said he wondered what it must be like to stand before a firing squad.

I told him I had seen a German general face one in Italy in December, 1945.

"Did he do it bravely?" Robert Frost asked.

I told him he had done it very bravely.

There was a television set in the corner and it seemed reasonable to ask if he took any interest in the medium.

"I do a little of it," he said, meaning being viewed, rather than viewing, "It's so when I see Peter at the gate, and he says 'Have you lived modern?' I can say 'I've flown and I've been on TV.'"

How about the Beat Generation?

"They're not even beat," said Robert Frost.

Robert Frost's America

Mark Van Doren

In the post–World War II years, poet and literary
critic Mark Van Doren wrote feature articles about
poetry for popular magazines like the *New Yorker*
and the *Atlantic Monthly*. In this article, Van Doren
examines the universality of Frost's poetry. Comparing Frost to such literary giants as Goethe, Homer,
and Shakespeare, Van Doren argues that Frost's poems are not dependent on understanding a particular location. He claims that Frost is successful in part
because there is substance behind the pleasure his
poems give: "He does not parade his learning, and
may in fact not know that he has it: but there in his
poems it is, and it is what makes them so solid, so
humorous, and so satisfying."

Robert Frost has been discovering America all his life. He
has also been discovering the world; and since he is a really
wise poet, the one thing has been the same thing as the
other. He is more than a New England poet; he is more than
an American poet; he is a poet who can be understood anywhere by readers versed in matters more ancient and universal than the customs of one country, whatever that country is. Frost's country is the country of human sense: of
experience, of imagination, and of thought. His poems start
at home, as all good poems do; as Homer's did, as Shakespeare's, as Goethe's, and as Baudelaire's; but they end up
everywhere, as only the best poems do. This is partly because his wisdom is native to him, and could not have been
suppressed by any circumstance; it is partly, too, because his
education has been right. He is our least provincial poet because he is the best grounded in those ideas—Greek, He-
brew, modern European and even Oriental—which make
for well-built art at any time. He does not parade his learning, and may in fact not know that he has it: but there in his

Reprinted from Mark Van Doren, "Robert Frost's America," *The Atlantic Monthly*, June
1951, with the permission of Charles and John Van Doren.

poems it is, and it is what makes them so solid, so humorous, and so satisfying.

His many poems have been different from one another and yet alike. They are the work of a man who has never stopped exploring himself—or, if you like, America, or better yet, the world. He has been able to believe, as any good artist must, that the things he knows best because they are his own will turn out to be true for other people. He trusts his own feelings, his own doubts, his own certainties, his own excitements. And there is absolutely no end to these, given the skill he needs to state them and the strength never to be wearied by his subject matter. . . .

Frost is more and more read, by old readers and by young, because in this crucial and natural sense he has so much to say. He is a generous poet. His book confides many discoveries, and shares with its readers a world as wild as it is wide—a dangerous world, hard to live in, yet the familiar world that is the only one we shall ever have, and that we can somehow love for the bad things in it as well as the good, the unintelligible as well as the intelligible.

Frost is a laconic New Englander: that is to say, he talks more than anybody. He talks all the time. The inhabitants of New England accuse one another of talking too much, but all are guilty together, all are human; for man is a talking animal, and never more so than when he is trying to prove that silence is best. Frost has expressed the virtue of silence in hundreds of poems, each one of them more ingenious than the last in the way it takes of suggesting that it should not have been written at all. The greatest people keep still.

> There may be little or much beyond the grave,
> But the strong are saying nothing until they see.

Joking aside, Frost is a generous giver. He is not, thank heaven, one of those exiguous modern poets . . . who hope to be loved because they have delivered so little: the fewer the poems the better the poet. The fact is that the greatest poets have been, among other things, prolific: they have had much to say, and nothing has prevented them from keeping at it till they died.

Contrary to a certain legend, good poets get better with age, as Thomas Hardy for another instance did. The *Collected Poems* of Hardy are a universe through which the reader may travel forever, entertained as he goes by the same paradox as that which appears in the *Complete Poems* of Frost: the universe in question is presented as a grim, bleak place, but the longer one stares at it the warmer it seems, and the more capable of justifying itself beneath the stars. By an almost illicit process it manages in the end to sing sweetly of itself—not sentimentally, or as if it leaned upon illusion, but with a deep sweetness that truth cannot disturb. For truth is in the sweetness: a bittersweetness, shall we say, but all the better preserved for being so.

And this is the case, whether with Hardy or with Frost, because the poet has never grown tired of his function; has always known more, and known it better, as time passed; and has found it the most natural thing in the world to say so in new terms.

> My object in living is to unite
> My avocation and my vocation.

The poet in Frost has never been different from the man, or the man from the poet; he has lived in his poetry at the same time that he has lived outside of it, and neither life has interfered with the other. Indeed it has helped; which is why we know that his poems mean exactly what he means, and might say in some other language if he chose. But he has chosen this language as the most personal he could find, toward the end that what it conveys should be personal for us too. We need not agree with everything he says in order to think him wise. It is rather that he sounds and feels wise, because he is sure of what he knows. And the extent of what he knows would never be guessed by one who met him only in anthologies. He is powerful there, but in the *Complete Poems* we find a universe of many recesses, and few readers have found their way into all of these. Some of them are very narrow, it would seem, and out of the ordinary way; in the language of criticism they might even be dismissed as little "conceits"; but the narrowest of them is likely to lead further in than we suspected, toward the central room where Frost's understanding is at home.

The sign that he is at home is that his language is plain; it is the human vernacular, as simple on the surface as monosyllables can make it. Strangely enough this is what makes some readers say he is hard—he is always referring to things he does not name, at any rate in the long words they suppose proper. He seems to be saying less than he does; it is only when we read close and listen well, and think between the sentences, that we become aware of what his poems are about. What they are about is the important thing—more important, we are tempted to think, than the words themselves, though it was the words that brought the subject on. The subject is the world: a huge and ruthless place which men will never quite understand, any more than they will understand themselves; and yet it is the same old place that men have always been trying to understand, and to this extent it is as familiar as an old boot or an old back door, lovable for what it is in spite of the fact that it does not speak up and identify itself in the idiom of abstraction. Frost is a philosopher, but his ideas are behind his poems, not in them—buried well, for us to guess at if we please. . . .

CONTRADICTIONS AND LEARNING TO BE STILL

We know nothing of justice if we know nothing of strife. It is tension that maintains our equilibrium; if opposites could not feel each other in the dark there would be no possibility of light. Good fences make good neighbors—each knows where he is and what confines him. Without a wall between them, each would confuse himself with the other and cease to exist; or if there were fighting, it would be too close—a mere scramble, in which neither party could be made out. Distance is a good thing, and so is admitted difference, even when it sounds like hostility. For there can be a harmony of separate sounds that seem to be at war with another, but one sound is like no sound at all, or else it is like death. Let each thing know its limits even as it strains to pass them. No limit will ever be passed, since indeed it is a limit. Which does not mean that we shall never stare across the void between ourselves and others. People, for instance, who look at the sea—

> They cannot look out far,
> They cannot look in deep.
> But when was that ever a bar
> To any watch they keep?

It is human to want to know more than we can. But it is most human to know what "cannot" means.

Frost never says these things either; his poems only suggest them, and suggest further things that contradict them. His muse, like the truth, is cantankerous; it keeps on turning up fresh evidence against itself. And yet we cannot miss the always electric presence of opposition—two things or persons staring at each other across some kind of wall. Frost has no interest in doors that do not lock, in friends who do not know they are enemies too, or in enemies who do not know how to pretend they are friends, and even believe it as far as things can go. His drumlin woodchuck sits forth from his habitation like one who invites the world to come and visit him; but he never forgets the two-door burrow at his back. So Frost himself can reflect upon the triple bronze that guards him from infinity: his skin, his house, and his country. If he is greatly interested in the stars, and no poet is more so, the reason is that they are another world which he can see from this one, and accept or challenge as the mood of the moment dictates. They burn in their places as he burns in his, and it is just as well that neither fire can consume the other; yet each of them is a fire, and secretly longs to mingle with its far neighbor.

The great thing about man for Frost is that he has the

REMARKS AT AMHERST COLLEGE

John F. Kennedy was the first president to commission a poem for his inauguration. Here, Kennedy contends that Frost's faith in the spirit of man gives us all reason to hope for the future of America.

Frost was one of the granite figures of our time in America. He was supremely two things: an artist and an American. A nation reveals itself not only by the men it produces but also by the men it honors, the men it remembers. . . .

He brought an unsparing instinct for reality to bear on the platitudes and pieties of society. His sense of the human tragedy fortified him against self-deception and easy consolation. "I have been," he wrote, "one acquainted with the night." And because he knew the midnight as well as the high noon, because he understood the ordeal as well as the triumph of the human spirit, he gave his age strength with which to overcome despair. At bottom, he held a deep faith in the spirit of man, and it is hardly an accident that Robert Frost coupled poetry and power, for he saw poetry as the means of saving power from itself. When power leads men towards arrogance, poetry reminds him of his limitations. When power narrows the areas of man's concern, poetry reminds him of the richness and diversity of his existence. When power corrupts, poetry cleanses. For art establishes the basic human truth which must serve as the touchstone of our judgment.

John Fitzgerald Kennedy, "Remarks at Amherst College." Speech given in Amherst, Massachusetts, October 26, 1963.

power of standing still where he is. He is on the earth, and it is only one of many places, and perhaps every other place is better. But this is his place, where in spite of his longing to leave it he can stay till his time comes. Like any other distinguished person, Frost lives in two worlds at once: this one, and another one which only makes it more attractive. The superiority of the other one is what proves the goodness of the one we have, which doggedly we keep on loving, as doggedly it tolerates and educates us if we let it do so. Wisdom is enduring it exactly as it is; courage is being familiar with it and afraid of it in the right proportions; temperance is the skill to let it be; and justice is the knowledge that between it and you there will always be a lover's quarrel, never to die into cold silence and never to be made up. The main thing is the mutual respect.

Excerpt from "The Road Taken"

Derek Walcott

Pulitzer Prize–winning poet and playwright Derek Walcott teaches English and poetry at Boston University. In this selection, Walcott contrasts the rugged public persona of Frost with the private, careful disciplinarian.

In 1912, when he was thirty-eight, Frost left Boston with his family for England, to devote himself to writing. He submitted *A Boy's Will*, his first collection, to the English publisher David Nutt, and it was accepted. He lived in a cottage in Buckinghamshire. In London, at Harold Munro's Poetry Bookshop, he met the poet F.S. Flint, who introduced him to Ezra Pound. Pound gave *A Boy's Will* a good review because, for all his aggressive cosmopolitanism and campaigning for the classics and "the new," Pound was as much a vernacular regional poet as Frost, and the genuine Americanness of Frost must have stirred a patriotic claim in him as much as the tonal authenticity of Eliot did. He derided the falsely modern and saw a classic shape in Frost that made "it" (poetry) new by its directness and its vigor: Frost's writing achieved a vernacular elation in tone, not with the cheap device of dialect spelling or rustic vocabulary, but with a clean ear and a fresh eye. (Pound found the same qualities in Hemingway.) And Yeats told Pound that *A Boy's Will* was "the best poetry written in America for a long time." The judgment remains right.

It was in England, in discussions with Flint and T.E. Hulme, that Frost clarified his direction by "the sounds of sense with all their irregularity of accent across the regular beat of the metre." Pound's encouragement—or, better, his papal benediction—turned into belligerence. Frost calls Pound a "quasi-friend" and writes: "He says I must write something much more like *vers libre* or he will let me perish by neglect. He really threatens." He worries that Pound's good review of *North of Boston* will describe him as one of Pound's "party of American literary refugees." (Later, down the years, down their different roads, Frost petitioned against Pound's imprisonment, even if he was enraged at the award of the Bollingen Prize to him; and Pound himself had no choice but to recognize the syntactical variety in Frost's verse, the *vers libre* within the taut frame.)

Frost's early mastery of stress looks natural. A deftness, like a skipping stone, evades the predictable scansion by a sudden parenthesis, by a momentarily forgotten verb—"that laid the swale in rows . . . and scared a bright green snake," and shifting, dancing caesuras.

Anything more than the truth would have seemed too weak
To the earnest love that laid the swale in rows,
Not without feeble-pointed spikes of flowers
(Pale orchises), and scared a bright green snake.

Yet the dialogue of the dramatic poems is boxed in by a metrical rigidity that, strangely enough, is more stiff-backed than the narration, perhaps because these poems are thought of as one element of the whole poem rather than as theater, where narration recedes in the presence of action and the variety of individual voices solidifies the contradictions of melody character by character. "The Death of the Hired Man" and others are poems, and not plays, for this reason: the voice of the characters and their creator is one voice, Frost's, and one tone, something nearer to complaint and elegy than vocal conflict, the tragic edge instead of tragedy. It's as if all his characters were remembering poems by Robert Frost. From "A Hundred Collars":

"It's business, but I can't say it's not fun.
What I like best's the lay of different farms,
Coming out on them from a stretch of woods,
Or over a hill or round a sudden corner.
I like to find folks getting out in spring,
Raking the dooryard, working near the house."

A certain deadening of the ear had dated dramatic verse since the Victorians, who tried to resuscitate Elizabethan and Jacobean drama through the pentameter, prolonging a hollow, martial echo that could not render the ordinary and domestic, that did not take into account the charged and broken syntax of Webster or the late Shakespeare. The same reverential monody occurred in Victorian epic poetry. The Elizabethan echo had become part of the soaring architecture, a determination to be sublime that again divided the lyric from the dramatic voice, that took poetry away from the theater and back into the library. Frost felt that in New England he was being offered an unexplored, unuttered theater, away from the leaves of libraries, in a natural setting rich with stories and characters.

We think of Frost's work in theatrical terms, with the poet, of course, as its central character, mocking his crises, his stopping at a crossroads, but also because of the voices in the poems. These voices are American, but their meter is not as subtly varied as the lyrical and yet colloquial power of his own meditations. To read the "Masques," at least for this reader, is a duty, not a delight. One keeps wishing that they were plays, not theatrical poems. The vocabulary grows ornate:

> The myrrh tree gives it. Smell the rosin burning?
> The ornaments the Greek artificers
> Made for the Emperor Alexius . . .
> [. . .]
> And hark, the gold enameled nightingales
> Are singing.

The line is sometimes unspeakable:

> You poor, poor swallowable little man.

The humor is arch:

> Job: But, yes, I'm fine, except for now and then
> A reminiscent twinge of rheumatism.

"Vulgarity," the gift that comes from the mob, which great poetic dramatists possess, no matter how sublime their rhetoric, and which they need in order to force a single response from an audience, springs from the vernacular, from the oral rather than the written, and is based on popular banalities of humor and pathos—this power is what separates, say, Browning from Shakespeare, this eagerness to entertain, to put it crassly. With his own gifts of the vernacular and of self-dramatization, Frost might be expected to have produced a wide, popular theater, since the tone of American speech was ready and resolved. And yet, for all his winking and his intimacy, Frost is a very private poet.

When we imagine the single voice of Frost behind the lines, it is the sound of a personal vernacular, but heard as dialogue. The vernacular petrifies into the monodic, perhaps because the dramatic poem (is there a single really success-ful example in literature?) is a kind of mule, like the prose poem, and like the "Masques." The contradiction of any masque is the pitch of its diction; it is meant not to be acted but to be heard. Frost's theatrical dialogue has a monodic drone. Yeats, who in the beginning of his theatrical career was as dutiful to the pentameter as Frost remained, finally broke away from it vehemently and triumphantly in "Purga-tory," and he did so with a rapid and common diction that came from the pub and the street, until the lyric and dra-matic pitch were one sound, as it is with the Jacobeans. In Frost's poetical theater, the diction becomes stately, working almost against the accent. It was not a betrayal or a defeat but a matter of temperament. Frost's temperament was too hermetic for the theater.

But something wonderful, revolutionary within the con-vention, happened to Frost's ear between *A Boy's Will* and *North of Boston.* He wrote American, without vehement chal-lenge. He wrote free or syllabic verse within the deceptive margins of the pentameter. He played tennis, to use his fa-mous description, but you couldn't see the net; his caesuras slid with a wry snarl over the surface, over the apparently conventional scansion.

Something there is that doesn't love a wall . . .

appears, to eye and ear, to be:

Some / thing / there is / that doesn't / love / a wall . . .

That is certainly how it would sound in English, to the Geor-gian [native of Georgia in the former Soviet Union] ear. But think American. In that diction, parody is the basis of pro-nunciation, and there is only one caesura:

Something there is / that doesn't love a wall . . .

That rapid elision or slur of the second half of the line is as monumental a breakthrough for American verse as any ex-periment by Williams or cummings. It dislocates the pivot of traditional scansion; and the consequence is seismic but inimitable, because it is first of all Frost's voice, which in me-ter is first regional, then generic, eventually American. This happened with equal force to Yeats, but with Frost it is more alarming, since Yeats contracted the pentameter to octosyl-labics for propulsion's sake, for "that quarrel with others which we call rhetoric," for the purposes of political passion, but Frost achieved this upheaval within the pentameter. He accomplished it, that is, without making his meter as wry and sarcastic as Williams's, or as pyrotechnic as cummings's, or as solemn and portentous as Stevens's.

Once that confidence sprung to hand and voice, there was no other road for Frost but greatness, a greatness not of ambition but of vocation:

> Two roads diverged in a yellow wood,
> And sorry I could not travel both
> And be one traveler . . .

I am quoting from memory, which is the greatest tribute to poetry, and with some strain I could probably copy from the dictation of memory not only this poem but also several other poems of Frost's. For interior recitation, usually of complete poems, not only of lines or stanzas, Frost and Yeats, for their rhythm and design, are the most memorable poets of the century.

To fight against a predictable tone of incantation was a great task for the American. Yeats could ride the lilt and history of a long tradition. Frost was truly alone, and many of the poems dramatize his own singularity—not the romantic image of the neglected poet in a materialist society but the American romance of the pioneer, the inventor, the tinkerer (if the pentameter wasn't broken, why fix it?), who knows the rational needs of that society, one of which is the practicality of poetry, its workday occupation, the fusion of commerce and art, of carpentry and metrical composition, the "song of the open road." Whitman's vagabondage is romantic, perhaps even irresponsible. Frost stays put, close to stone walls, under apple orchards, mowing grass.

Excerpt from "Above the Brim"

Seamus Heaney

Seamus Heaney is an award-winning Irish poet and poet-in-residence at Harvard University. In this selection, Heaney explores the dark side of Frost's country scenes and his use of sound and sense to reflect this darkness. Heaney contends that Robert Frost is so talented and skillful that reading his poetry is like being offered a glass so ample that it practically overflows: supremely generous, but never sloppy.

Among major poets of the English language in this century, Robert Frost is the one who takes the most punishment. "Like a chimpanzee" is how one friend of mine remembers him in the flesh, but in the afterlife of the text he has been consigned to a far less amiable sector of the bestiary, among the stoats perhaps, or the weasels. Calculating self-publicist, reprehensible egotist, oppressive parent—theories of the death of the author have failed to lay the ghost of this vigorous old contender who beats along undauntedly at the reader's elbow. His immense popular acclaim during his own lifetime; his apotheosis into an idol mutually acceptable to his own and his country's self-esteem, and greatly inflationary of both; his constantly resourceful acclimatization of himself to this condition, as writer and performer—it all generated a critical resistance and fed a punitive strain which is never far to seek in literary circles anyhow.

Still, it would be wrong to see this poet as the unwitting victim of the fashion which he surfed upon for decades. Demonically intelligent, as acute about his own masquerades as he was about others', Frost obeyed the ancient command to know himself. Like [William Butler] Yeats at the end of "Dialogue of Self and Soul," Frost would be "content to live

Excerpted from "Above the Brim," by Seamus Heaney, from *Homage to Robert Frost*, by Joseph Brodsky, Seamus Heaney, and Derek Walcott. Copyright ©1996 by the Estate of Joseph Brodsky, Seamus Heaney, and Derek Walcott. Reprinted by permission of Farrar, Straus & Giroux, Inc.

it all again," and be content also to "cast out remorse." Unlike Yeats, however, he would expect neither a flow of sweetness into his breast nor a flash of beatitude upon the world to ensue from any such bout of self-exculpation. He made no secret of the prejudice and contrariness at the center of his nature, and never shirked the bleakness of that last place in himself. He was well aware of the abrasiveness of many of his convictions and their unpopular implications in the context of [Franklin Roosevelt's] New Deal politics, yet for all his archness, he did not hide those convictions or retreat from them.

Frost's appetite for his own independence was fierce and expressed itself in a reiterated belief in his right to limits: his defenses, his fences, and his freedom were all interdependent. Yet he also recognized that his compulsion to shape his own destiny and to proclaim the virtues of self-containment arose from a terror of immense, unlimited, and undefined chaos. This terror gets expressed melodramatically in a poem like "Design," and obliquely in a poem like "Provide, Provide," but it is also there in many of his more casual pronouncements. Here he is, for example, writing to Amy Bonner in June 1937:

> There are no two things as important to us in life and art as being threatened and being saved. What are ideals of form for if we aren't going to be made to fear for them? All our ingenuity is lavished on getting into danger legitimately so that we may be genuinely rescued.

Frost believed, in other words, that individual venture and vision arose as a creative defense against emptiness, and that it was therefore always possible that a relapse into emptiness would be the ultimate destiny of consciousness. If good fences made good neighbors, if ... a certain callousness of self-assertion was part of the price of adjusting to reality, Frost was ready to pay that price in terms of exclusiveness and isolation, and in terms also of guardedness and irony. ... The main thing is that Frost was prepared to look without self-deception into the crystal of indifference in himself where his moral and artistic improvisations were both prefigured and scrutinized, and in this essay I shall be concerned to show that his specifically poetic achievement is profoundly guaranteed and resilient because it is "genuinely rescued" from negative recognitions, squarely faced, and abidingly registered.

Frost was always ready to hang those negative recognitions in the balance against his more comfortable imaginings. He made it clear, for example, that there was a cold shadow figure behind the warm-blooded image of his generally beloved horseman in "Stopping by Woods on a Snowy Evening":

> My little horse must think it queer
> To stop without a farmhouse near
> Between the woods and frozen lake
> The darkest evening of the year.
>
> He gives his harness bells a shake
> To ask if there is some mistake.
> The only other sound's the sweep
> Of easy wind and downy flake.

This rider, faring forward against the drift of more than snow, a faithful, self-directed quester with promises to keep and miles to go before he sleeps, this figure finds his counterpart in "Desert Places," a poem of the same length, written in almost the same rhyme scheme. In "Desert Places" Frost implicitly concedes the arbitrariness of the consolations offered by the earlier poem and deliberately undermines its sureties. The social supports that were vestigially present in "promises to keep" have now been pulled away, and the domestic security of woods with owners in the village is rendered insignificant by a vacuous interstellar immensity:

> Snow falling and night falling fast, oh, fast
> In a field I looked into going past,
> And the ground almost covered smooth in snow,
> But a few weeds and stubble showing last.
>
> The woods around it have it—it is theirs.
> All animals are smothered in their lairs.
> I am too absent-spirited to count;
> The loneliness includes me unawares.
>
> And lonely as it is that loneliness
> Will be more lonely ere it will be less—
> A blanker whiteness of benighted snow
> With no expression, nothing to express.
>
> They cannot scare me with their empty spaces
> Between stars—on stars where no human race is.
> I have it in me so much nearer home
> To scare myself with my own desert places.

This poem gives access to the dark side of Frost, which was always there behind the mask of Yankee hominess, a side of him which also became fashionable late in the day, after [critic] Lionel Trilling gave it the modernists' blessing in a speech at Frost's eighty-fifth birthday party. Trilling there drew attention to Frost's Sophoclean gift for making the neuter outback of experience scrutable in a way that privileges neither the desolate unknown nor the human desire to shelter from it. I am going to pause with the poem at this early stage, however, not in order to open the vexed question of Frost's dimensions as a philosophical writer or to address the range of his themes or to contextualize his stances, imaginative and civic, within American political and intellectual history. All of these things are worth considering, but I raise them only to salute them dutifully and so pass on to my own particular area of interest.

This arises from a lifetime of pleasure in Frost's poems as events in language, flaunts and vaunts full of projective force and deliquescent backwash, the crestings of a tide that lifts all spirits. Frost may have indeed declared that his whole anxiety was for himself as a performer, but the performance succeeded fully only when it launched itself beyond skill and ego into a run of energy that brimmed up outside the poet's conscious intention and control.

Consider, for example, the conclusion of "Desert Places," which I have just quoted: "I have it in me so much nearer home / To scare myself with my own desert places." However these lines may incline toward patness, whatever risk they run of making the speaker seem to congratulate himself too easily as an initiate of darkness, superior to the deluded common crowd, whatever trace they contain of knowingness that mars other poems by Frost, they still succeed convincingly. They overcome one's incipient misgivings and subsume them into the larger, more impersonal, and undeniable emotional occurrence which the whole poem represents.

Frost as a Terrifying Poet

Lionel Trilling

Lionel Trilling was a figurehead of the New York
City social scene during the 1950s and 1960s, attending social events and writing about everything from
literature to trends. He was one of the first critics to
look deeply into Frost's work and see the dark
themes beneath the rustic settings. Trilling argues
that nothing is sweet or nostalgic about Frost: He is
modern, jarring, and terrifying.

I have to say that my Frost—*my Frost:* what airs we give ourselves when once we believe that we have come into posses-
sion of a poet!—I have to say that my Frost is not the Frost I
seem to perceive existing in the minds of so many of his ad-
mirers. He is not the Frost who confounds the characteristically modern practice of poetry by his notable democratic
simplicity of utterance: on the contrary. He is not the Frost
who controverts the bitter modern astonishment at the nature of human life: the opposite is so. He is not the Frost who
reassures us by his affirmation of old virtues, simplicities,
pieties, and ways of feeling: anything but. I will not go so far
as to say that my Frost is not essentially an American poet at
all: I believe that he is quite as American as everyone thinks
he is, but not in the way that everyone thinks he is.

In the matter of the Americanism of American literature
one of my chief guides is that very remarkable critic, D.H.
Lawrence. Here are the opening sentences of Lawrence's
great outrageous book about classic American literature.
"We like to think of the old fashioned American classics as
children's books. Just childishness on our part. The old
American art speech contains an alien quality which belongs to the American continent and to nowhere else." And
this unique alien quality, Lawrence goes on to say, the world

From Lionel Trilling, "A Speech on Robert Frost: A Cultural Episode." Copyright
©1959 by Lionel Trilling. Reprinted with the permission of The Wylie Agency, Inc.
First published in *The Partisan Review,* Summer 1959.

has missed. "It is hard to hear a new voice," he says, "as hard as to listen to an unknown language. . . . Why? Out of fear. The world fears a new experience more than it fears anything. It can pigeonhole any idea. But it can't pigeonhole a real new experience. It can only dodge. The world is a great dodger, and the Americans the greatest. Because they dodge their own very selves." I should like to pick up a few more of Lawrence's sentences, feeling the freer to do so because they have an affinity to Mr. Frost's prose manner and substance: "An artist is usually a damned liar, but his art, if it be art, will tell you the truth of his day. And that is all that matters. Away with eternal truth. Truth lives from day to day. . . . The old American artists were hopeless liars. . . . Never trust the artist. Trust the tale. The proper function of the critic is to save the tale from the artist who created it. . . . Now listen to me, don't listen to him. He'll tell you the lie you expect, which is partly your fault for expecting it."

Now in point of fact Robert Frost is *not* a liar. I would not hesitate to say that he was if I thought he was. But no, he is not. In certain of his poems—I shall mention one or two in a moment—he makes it perfectly plain what he is doing; and if we are not aware of what he is doing in other of his poems, where he is not quite so plain, that is not his fault but our own. It is not from him that the tale needs to be saved.

I conceive that Robert Frost is doing in his poems what Lawrence says the great writers of the classic American tradition did. That enterprise of theirs was of an ultimate radicalism. It consisted, Lawrence says, of two things: a disintegration and sloughing off of the old consciousness, by which Lawrence means the old European consciousness, and the forming of a new consciousness underneath.

THE TERRIBLE ACTUALITIES OF LIFE

So radical a work, I need scarcely say, is not carried out by reassurance, nor by the affirmation of old virtues and pieties. It is carried out by the representation of the terrible actualities of life in a new way. I think of Robert Frost as a terrifying poet. Call him, if it makes things any easier, a tragic poet, but it might be useful every now and then to come out from under the shelter of that literary word. The universe that he conceives is a terrifying universe. Read the poem called "Design" and see if you sleep the better for it. Read "Neither Out Far nor In Deep," which often seems to me the most perfect poem of our time, and see if you are warmed by anything in it except the energy with which emptiness is perceived.

But the *people,* it will be objected, the *people* who inhabit this possibly terrifying universe! About them there is nothing that can terrify; surely the people in Mr. Frost's poems can only reassure us by their integrity and solidity. Perhaps so. But I cannot make the disjunction. It may well be that ultimately they reassure us in some sense, but first they terrify us, or should. We must not be misled about them by the curious tenderness with which they are represented, a tenderness which extends to a recognition of the tenderness which they themselves can often give. But when ever have people been so isolated, so lightning-blasted, so tried down and calcined by life, so reduced, each in his own way, to some last irreducible core of being. Talk of the disintegration and sloughing off of the old consciousness! The people of Robert Frost's poems have done that with a vengeance. Lawrence says that what the Americans refused to accept was "the post-Renaissance humanism of Europe," "the old European spontaneity," "the flowing easy humor of Europe" and that seems to me a good way to describe the people who inhabit Robert Frost's America. In the interests of what great other thing these people have made this rejection we cannot know for certain. But we can guess that it was in the interest of truth, of some truth of the self. This is what they all affirm by their humor (which is so *not* "the easy flowing humor of Europe"), by their irony, by their separateness and isolateness. They affirm *this* of themselves: that they are what they are, that this is their truth, and that if the truth be bare, as the truth often is, it is far better than a lie. For me the process by which they arrive at that truth is always terrifying. The manifest America of Mr. Frost's poems may be pastoral; the actual America is tragic.

Poetry as a Clarification of Life

W.H. Auden

W.H. Auden, the English poet and dramatist, was best known for his sophisticated and elaborate verse forms. Auden immigrated to the United States in 1939, becoming an American citizen, but he returned to Europe near the end of his life. In the following selection, Auden thoroughly examines Frost's poetry, which he deems modern in its subject matter and deceptively simple in its speech. Auden admires Frost, but he highlights the poet's limitations in this perceptive essay.

If asked who said *Beauty is Truth, Truth Beauty!,* a great many readers would answer "Keats." But Keats said nothing of the sort. It is what he said the Grecian Urn said, his description and criticism of a certain kind of work of art, the kind from which the evils and problems of this life, the "heart high sorrowful and cloyed," are deliberately excluded. The Urn, for example, depicts, among other beautiful sights, the citadel of a hill town; it does not depict warfare, the evil which makes the citadel necessary.

Art arises out of our desire for both beauty and truth and our knowledge that they are not identical. One might say that every poem shows some sign of a rivalry between Ariel and Prospero [from Shakespeare's *The Tempest*]; in every good poem their relation is more or less happy, but it is never without its tensions. The Grecian Urn states Ariel's position; Prospero's has been equally succinctly stated by Dr. Johnson: *The only end of writing is to enable the readers better to enjoy life or better to endure it.*

We want a poem to be beautiful, that is to say, a verbal earthly paradise, a timeless world of pure play, which gives us delight precisely because of its contrast to our historical existence with all its insoluble problems and inescapable suffering; at the same time we want a poem to be true, that is to say, to provide us with some kind of revelation about our life which will show us what life is really like and free us from self-enchantment and deception, and a poet cannot bring us any truth without introducing into his poetry the problematic, the painful, the disorderly, the ugly. Though every poem involves *some* degree of collaboration between Ariel and Prospero, the role of each varies in importance from one poem to another: it is usually possible to say of a poem and, sometimes, of the whole output of a poet, that it is Ariel-dominated or Prospero-dominated. . . .

A PROSPERO-DOMINATED POET

Both in theory and practice Frost is a Prospero-dominated poet. In the preface to his *Collected Poems,* he writes:

> The sound is the gold in the ore. Then we will have the sound out alone and dispense with the inessential. We do till we make the discovery that the object in writing poetry is to make all poems sound as different as possible from each other, and the resources for that of vowels, consonants, punctuation, syntax, words, sentences, meter are not enough. We need the help of context—meaning—subject matter. . . . And we are back in poetry as merely one more art of having something to say, sound or unsound. Probably better if sound, because deeper and from wider experience. [A poem] begins in delight and ends in wisdom . . . a clarification of life—not necessarily a great clarification such as sects and cults are founded on, but in a momentary stay against confusion.

His poetic style is what I think Professor C. S. Lewis would call Good Drab. The music is always that of the speaking voice, quiet and sensible, and I cannot think of any other modern poet, except [Constantine] Cavafy, who uses language more simply. He rarely employs metaphors, and there is not a word, not a historical or literary reference in the whole of his work which would be strange to an unbookish boy of fifteen. Yet he manages to make this simple kind of speech express a wide variety of emotion and experience.

> Be that as may be, she was in their song.
> Moreover her voice upon their voices crossed
> Had now persisted in the woods so long
> That probably it would never be lost.
> Never again would bird's song be the same.
> And to do that to birds was why she came.

.   .   .   .   .   .

I hope if he is where he sees me now
He's so far off he can't see what I've come to.
You *can* come down from everything to nothing.
All is, if I'd a-known when I was young
And full of it, that this would be the end,
It doesn't seem as if I'd had the courage
To make so free and kick up in folk's faces.
I might have, but it doesn't seem as if.

The emotions in the first passage are tender, happy, and its reflections of a kind which could only be made by an educated man. The emotions in the second are violent and tragic, and the speaker a woman with no schooling. Yet the diction in both is equally simple. There are a few words the man uses which the woman would not use herself, but none she could not understand; her syntax is a little cruder than his, but only a little. Yet their two voices sound as distinct as they sound authentic.

 POETRY AND SCHOOL: HOW TO READ A POEM

In this excerpt from his Notebooks, *Robert Frost discusses how poems should be read.*

The way to read a poem in prose or verse is in the light of all the other poems ever written. We may begin anywhere. We *duff* into our first. We read that imperfectly (thoroughness with it would be fatal), but the better to read the second. We read the second the better to read the third, the third the better to read the fourth, the fourth the better to read the fifth, the fifth the better to read the first again, or the second if it so happens. For poems are not meant to be read in course any more than they are to be made a study of. I once made a resolve never to put any book to any use it wasn't intended for by its author. Improvement will not be a progression but a widening circulation. Our instinct is to settle down like a revolving dog and make ourselves at home among the poems, completely at our ease as to how they should be taken. The same people will be apt to take poems right as know how to take a hint when there is one and not to take a hint when none is intended. Theirs is the ultimate refinement.

We write in school chiefly because to try our hand at writing should make us better readers.

Almost everyone should almost have experienced the fact that a poem is an idea caught fresh in the act of dawning.

Robert Frost, "Poetry and School," *Atlantic Monthly*, June 4, 1951, pp. 30–31.

Frost's poetic speech is the speech of a mature mind, fully awake and in control of itself; it is not the speech of dream or of uncontrollable passion. Except in reported speech, interjections, imperatives and rhetorical interrogatives are rare. This does not mean, of course, that his poems are lacking in feeling; again and again, one is aware of strong, even violent, emotion behind what is actually said, but the saying is reticent, the poetry has, as it were, an auditory chastity. It would be impossible for Frost, even if he wished, to produce an unabashed roar of despair, as Shakespeare's tragic heroes so often can, but the man who wrote the following lines has certainly been acquainted with despair.

> I have stood still and stopped the sound of feet
> When far away an interrupted cry
> Came over houses from another street,
> But not to call me back or say good-bye.
> And further still at an unearthly height
> One luminary clock against the sky
> Proclaimed the time was neither wrong nor right.
> I have been one acquainted with the night.

Every style has its limitations.... A style, like Frost's, which approximates to ordinary speech is necessarily contemporary, the style of a man living in the first half of the twentieth century; it is not well suited, therefore, to subjects from the distant past, in which the difference between then and today is significant, or to mythical subjects which are timeless....

NATURAL SPEECH

Frost's tone of voice, even in his dramatic pieces, is that of a man talking to himself, thinking aloud and hardly aware of an audience. This manner is, of course, like all manners, calculated, and more sophisticated than most. The calculation is sound when the poems are concerned with personal emotions, but when the subject is one of public affairs or ideas of general interest, it may be a miscalculation. "Build Soil, a Political Pastoral" which Frost composed for the National Party Convention at Columbia University in 1932, was much criticized at the time by the Liberal-Left for being reactionary. Reading it today, one wonders what all their fuss was about, but the fireside-chat I'm-a-plain-fellow manner is still irritating. One finds oneself wishing that Columbia had invited [Irish poet William Butler] Yeats instead; he might have said the most outrageous things, but he would have put on a good act, and that is what we want from a poet when he speaks to us of what concerns us, not as private persons but as citizens. Perhaps Frost himself felt uneasy, for the last two lines of the poem, and the best, run thus:

We're too unseparate. And going home
From company means coming to our senses.

Any poetry which aims at being a clarification of life must be concerned with two questions about which all men, whether they read poetry or not, seek clarification.

1) *Who am I?* What is the difference between man and all other creatures? What relations are possible between them? What is man's status in the universe? What are the conditions of his existence which he must accept as his fate which no wishing can alter?

2) *Whom ought I to become?* What are the characteristics of the hero, the authentic man whom everybody should admire and try to become? Vice versa, what are the characteristics of the churl, the unauthentic man whom everybody should try to avoid becoming?

We all seek answers to these questions which shall be universally valid under all circumstances, but the experiences to which we put them are always local both in time and place. What any poet has to say about man's status in nature, for example, depends in part upon the landscape and climate he happens to live in and in part upon the reactions to it of his personal temperament. A poet brought up in the tropics cannot have the same vision as a poet brought up in Hertfordshire and, if they inhabit the same landscape, the chirpy social endomorph will give a different picture of it from that of the melancholic withdrawn ectomorph.

The nature in Frost's poetry is the nature of New England. New England is made of granite, is mountainous, densely wooded, and its soil is poor. It has a long severe winter, a summer that is milder and more pleasant than in most parts of the States, a short and sudden Spring, a slow and theatrically beautiful fall. Since it adjoins the eastern seaboard, it was one of the first areas to be settled but, as soon as the more fertile lands to the West were opened up, it began to lose population. Tourists and city dwellers who can afford a summer home may arrive for the summer, but much land which was once cultivated has gone back to the wild.

One of Frost's favorite images is the image of the abandoned house. In Britain or Europe, a ruin recalls either historical change, political acts like war or enclosure, or, in the case of abandoned mine buildings, a successful past which came to an end, not because nature was too strong, but because she had been robbed of everything she possessed. A ruin in Europe, therefore, tends to arouse reflections about human injustice and greed and the nemesis that overtakes human pride. But in Frost's poetry, a ruin is an image of human heroism, of a defense in the narrow pass against hopeless odds. . . .

A MALIGNANT NATURE

Thumbing through Frost's *Collected Poems,* I find twenty-one in which the season is winter as compared with five in which it is spring, and in two of these there is still snow on the ground; I find twenty-seven in which the time is night and seventeen in which the weather is stormy.

The commonest human situation in his poetry is of one man, or a man and wife, alone in a small isolated house in a snowbound forest after dark.

> Where I could think of no thoroughfare,
> Away on the mountain up far too high,
> A blinding headlight shifted glare
> And began to bounce down a granite stair
> Like a star fresh-fallen out of the sky,
> And I away in my opposite wood
> Am touched by that unintimate light
> And made feel less alone than I rightly should,
> For traveler there could do me no good
> Were I in trouble with night tonight.
>
>   .   .   .   .   .
>
> We looked and looked, but after all where are we?
> Do we know any better where we are,
> And how it stands between the night tonight
> And a man with a smokey lantern chimney,
> How different from the way it ever stood?

In "Two Look at Two," nature, as represented by a buck stag and a doe, responds in sympathy to man, as represented by a boy and girl, but the point of the poem is that this sympathetic response is a miraculous exception. The normal response is that described in "The Most of It."

> Some morning from the boulder-broken beach
> He would cry out on life that what it wants
> Is not its own love back in copy speech,
> But counter-love, original response.

And nothing ever came of what he cried
Unless it was the embodiment that crashed
In the cliff's talus on the other side,
And then in the far distant water splashed,
But after a time allowed for it to swim,
Instead of proving human when it neared
And some one else additional to him,
As a great buck it powerfully appeared . . .

Nature, however, is not to Frost, as she was to [writer Herman] Melville, malignant.

It must be a little more in favor of man,
Say a fraction of one per cent at least,
Or our number living wouldn't be steadily more.

She is . . . by her apparent indifference and hostility, even, calls forth all man's powers and courage and makes a real man of him.

Courage is not to be confused with romantic daring. It includes caution and cunning,

All we who prefer to live
Have a little whistle we give,
And flash at the least alarm
We dive down under the farm

and even financial prudence,

Better to go down dignified
With boughten friendship at your side
Than none at all. Provide, provide!

There have been European poets who have come to similar conclusions about the isolation of the human condition, and nature's indifference to human values, but, compared with an American, they are at a disadvantage in expressing them. Living as they do in a well, even overpopulated, countryside where, thanks to centuries of cultivation, Mother Earth has acquired human features, they are forced to make abstract philosophical statements or use uncommon atypical images, so that what they say seems to be imposed upon them by theory and temperament rather than by facts. An American poet like Frost, on the other hand, can appeal to facts for which any theory must account and which any temperament must admit.

The Frostian man is isolated not only in space but also in time. In Frost's poems the nostalgic note is seldom, if ever, struck. When he writes a poem about childhood like "Wild Grapes," childhood is not seen as a magical Eden which will all too soon, alas, be lost, but as a school in which the first lessons of adult life are learned. The setting of one of his best long poems, "The Generations of Man," is the ancestral home of the Stark family in the town of Bow, New Hampshire. Bow is a rock-strewn township where farming has fallen off and sproutlands flourish since the axe has gone. The Stark family mansion is by now reduced to an old cellar-hole at the side of a by-road. The occasion described in the poem is a gathering together from all over of the Stark descendants, an advertising stunt thought up by the governor of the state. The characters are a boy Stark and a girl Stark, distant cousins, who meet at the cellar-hole and are immediately attracted to each other. Their conversation turns, naturally, to their common ancestors, but, in fact, they know nothing about them. The boy starts inventing stories and doing imaginary imitations of their voices as a way of courtship, making their ancestors hint at marriage and suggest building a new summer home on the site of the old house. The real past, that is to say, is unknown and unreal to them; its role in the poem is to provide a lucky chance for the living to meet. . . .

American Characteristics

Every poet is at once a representative of his culture and its critic. Frost has never written satires, but it is not hard to guess what, as an American, he approves and disapproves of in his own countrymen. The average American is a stoic and, contrary to what others are apt to conclude from his free-and-easy friendly manner, reticent, far more reticent than the average Englishman about showing his feelings. He believes in independence because he has to; life is too mobile and circumstances change too fast for him to be supported by any fixed frame of family or social relations. In a crisis he will help his neighbor, whoever he may be, but he will regard someone who is always coming for help as a bad neighbor, and he disapproves of all self-pity and nostalgic regret. All these qualities find their expression in Frost's poetry, but there are other American characteristics which are not to be found there, the absence of which implies disapproval; the belief, for instance, that it should be possible, once the right gimmick has been found, to build the New Jerusalem on earth in half an hour. One might describe Frost as a Tory, provided that one remembers that all American political parties are Whigs.

CHAPTER 2

The Theme of Nature

READINGS ON
ROBERT FROST

Frost's Depictions of Rural Life

John F. Lynen

John F. Lynen explains why Frost used so many scenes of pastoral life in his poems in this excerpt from his book, *The Pastoral Art of Robert Frost.* Although the settings are rural, Lynen contends that they are also complex.

Frost discovered a new myth of rural life. . . . As a poet Frost matured late; his early verse reveals a constant searching for an idiom and a subject. From the beginning his instincts drew him towards rural subjects, but in the long period of experiment we find him writing of these in an elegant manner reminiscent of late Victorian nature poetry. Only when he learned to adopt the perspective of pastoral and wrote from the point of view of an actual New England farmer did he come into his own as an artist. The change was a sudden one; it occurred when his imagination grasped the poetic possibilities of the region he knew so well, when, by leaving home for a brief sojourn in old England, he came to see in the life of rural New England a remote, ideal world which could serve the same function as Arcadia. The important role of regionalism in Frost's poetry is a large subject, and we will therefore have to explore his myth of New England more fully later on. For the moment, let us accept it as a myth. Our present purpose is to consider somewhat further the kind of poetry it makes possible.

Frost, like the writers of old pastoral, draws upon our feeling that the rural world is representative of human life in general. By working from this nodal idea he is able to develop in his poems a very broad range of reference without ever seeming to depart from particular matters of fact. He says nothing of other places and other times—he gives us only the minute particulars of his own immediate experience; yet, as we have seen in "Stopping by Woods," the things described seem everywhere to point beyond the rural world. The effect is to create a remarkable depth of reference. One senses a powerful symbolism at work in the poem, but when one attempts to specify just what the images refer to their meaning proves too delicate, too elusive to capture. One can define the poem's meaning in general terms, as I have done, but this is not entirely satisfactory. Such a definition can give only a flat, abstract statement of theme, whereas the beauty of such poetry consists in the presence of manifold particular references lurking behind the symbols.

A symbolism of this kind is neither defined by traditional references nor shaped through such devices as metaphor, but emerges, like the three dimensional effects of painting, from the very perspective of the poet's vision. Pastoralism, as we have noted, is characterized by a basic duality: it portrays rural life, but it always does this with reference to the great world beyond. Its essential technique is that of creating a sharp contrast between the two. The pastoral poet tends to emphasize the great distance which separates the shepherd from the aristocrat and the rustic setting from the city and court. His method is paradoxical in that his intent is to portray universal experience by revealing the basic realities common to both worlds, yet he achieves this by insisting upon their dissimilarity. If the country is to become the microcosm of the great world it must be pictured as a little world in itself, one which is separate from the realm of ordinary experience even though, in another sense, it displays the familiar reality. It is, then, by making his Arcadia remote that the pastoral poet transforms it into a symbolic world. And since the rustic scene in its entirety is taken as representative of all other levels of being, the things that belong to it—the shepherds and farmers, their tasks, amusements, and concerns, the simple objects familiar to them and the scenic aspects of their surroundings—are all infused with symbolic suggestions.

AN ALTERNATE TO URBANITY

It is just such a perspective and such a method of pastoral contrast that gives the simple scenes and episodes Frost describes their extraordinary breadth of reference. When one considers his Yankee poems, one begins to notice a number of fundamental similarities between them and the old pastorals. His New England, like Arcadia, is a distinct plane of existence portrayed in such a way that a comparison with the outer world is always strongly implied. It is isolated from ordinary experience, a society with its own folkways, customs, and ideals, a locality with its own distinctive landscape. Like the old pastoralists, he emphasizes the uniqueness of his rural world. It is an agrarian society isolated within an urbanized world, and its country folk are separated from the modern reading public by a gulf of social, cultural, and economic differences nearly as broad as that dividing the swain of the old pastoral from the courtly reader. If the awareness of class differences, which is so prominent in traditional eclogues, is necessarily much less important in Frost's pastorals, regionalism provides another means for creating the effect of remoteness. He sets his rural world apart by stressing its distinctly local traits and portraying Yankee life as quite different from that in the cosmopolitan urban society. And as in the old pastoral, awareness of differences leads to a recognition of parallels. The more unusual and remote from everyday life his rural New England appears, the more effectively he can use it as a medium for the symbolic representation of realities in other areas of experience.

Frost's method as pastoral poet is nicely illustrated by one of his most familiar lyrics, "The Pasture." This poem is of particular interest in that the poet has for many years used it as the epigraph for editions of his collected verse, a fact which suggests that he regards it as a symbol of the kind of poetry he writes. "The Pasture" may at first appear very simple indeed, since the materials of which it is composed are so slight. It seems merely to describe a few casual details of farm life which the poet sees in going about his tasks. But as in "Stopping by Woods," the bits of description somehow cohere to form a pattern which expresses a much broader meaning than is overtly stated. It is important to note that the poem is an invitation: the poet invites someone, perhaps a person he loves, perhaps just a friend, to come with him and see the glimpses of delicate beauty to be found in the pasture. The implication is that the person invited knows little of such things. More important, he will have to be initiated into the special way of looking at them which makes them precious and meaningful. The leaves floating in the pasture spring, the little calf, so young it totters when its mother licks

it, have the simplicity and innocence of pristine reality, and
the poem implies that the average person, like the person invited, could not see the beauty in such natural, everyday
things without the poet as guide. To appreciate these, he will
have to abandon knowledge as the great world understands
it and learn to adopt the poet's special way of seeing.

RURALITY AFFECTS "VISION"

The poet's invitation is really to a kind of vision, and this vision is to be understood through its implicit difference from
the common view of reality. But the invitation is also to a
place, the pasture itself, for only within the humble, out-of-
the-way rural world is this special mode of perception possible. The pasture, then, is both the subject of the vision and
its perspective; the mode of perception is embodied in the
images themselves. For all its sweetness the poem is not
tainted by sentimentality, because while it describes the
charming aspects of the pasture, it is concerned less with
beauty for its own sake than with the organic wholeness
which makes this beauty meaningful. Frost's theme here is
the coherence of the rural scene, the unity between the
things observed and the way of seeing, between objects and
thought, between man's work—the speaker of the poem
must clean the spring and fetch the young calf—and his aes-
thetic experience. This unity raises the world of the pasture
above other realms of human life by showing it as an ordered world where the significance of things is simple and
apparent. This is manifest in the symbols themselves: the
spring and the calf represent the source, the simple, pure,
innocent beginnings of things. . . .

The broad and generalized symbolism characteristic of
pastoral results from the fact that the pastoral analogy is implied, rather than stated. While the pastoral poet deals with
the great world as well as the rural, he does so indirectly.
What he actually portrays is country life. The area extending
beyond the limits of his Arcadia serves as a background
against which the rural subject is seen in clear silhouette;
and precisely because this larger world is never explicitly
defined, the rustic scene can represent many other levels of
being. Such use of analogy makes the difficulty of interpret-
ing Frost's poetry understandable; it explains why his symbolism, though strongly felt, is always hard to tie down to
specific referents. The scenes he portrays do not point to-

ward particular things in other contexts, but rather represent whole classes of experience and types of things. We see this immediately when we attempt to specify what such images as the woods filled with snow in "Stopping by Woods" or the newborn calf in "The Pasture" symbolize. We can say that the woods represent a kind of temptation to indulge the imagination and that the calf suggests birth, fertility, and natural innocence, but beyond this one cannot safely go. In other words, we can delimit the general area of meaning behind the symbol, but this area contains an indefinite number of referents, none of which can be chosen as *the* right one. Of course, in all good poetry symbolic meaning will be manifold and ambiguous, but in Frost's it tends to be so broad as to seem indefinite. . . .

His poetry, however, has its own kind of precision. While the referents of his symbols are not specified, the *area* within which referents are to be found is strictly delimited. . . . In Frost the symbol, presented quite casually as an image, opens outward upon a vista of meaning. The vista does not have any definite terminus and in the farthest distance fades into vague areas of suggestion. What is definite is the *line* of vision, the direction.

"MENDING WALL"

In "Mending Wall," for example, the difficulties raised by Frost's mode of symbolism are apparent. The poem seems merely descriptive and anecdotal in character, yet everyone who has read it will remember a certain feeling of puzzlement, a sense that Frost is driving at some point which one is not quite able to grasp. We are told how the speaker in the poem and his neighbor get together every spring to repair the stone wall between their properties. The neighbor, a crusty New England farmer, seems to have a deep-seated faith in the value of walls. He declines to explain his belief and will only reiterate his father's saying, "Good fences make good neighbors." The speaker is of the opposite opinion. As he points out:

> There where it is we do not need the wall:
> He is all pine and I am apple orchard.

To him the neighbor's adherence to his father's saying suggests the narrowness and blind habit of the primitive:

> He moves in darkness as it seems to me,
> Not of woods only and the shade of trees.

Yet the speaker's own attitude is also enigmatic and in some respects primitive. He seems to be in sympathy with some elemental spirit in nature which denies all boundaries:

Something there is that doesn't love a wall,
That sends the frozen-ground-swell under it,
And spills the upper boulders in the sun:
And makes gaps even two can pass abreast. . . .

No one has seen them made or heard them made,
But at spring mending-time we find them there. . . .

Something there is that doesn't love a wall,
That wants it down. I could say 'Elves' to him,
But it's not elves exactly, and I'd rather
He said it for himself.

The poem portrays a clash between these two points of view, and it may therefore seem that its meaning is the solution Frost offers to the disagreement. The poem leads one to ask, which is right, the speaker or his Yankee neighbor? Should man tear down the barriers which isolate individuals from one another, or should he recognize that distinctions and limits are necessary to human life? Frost does not really provide an answer, and the attempt to wrest one from his casual details and enigmatic comments would falsify his meaning. It is not Frost's purpose to convey a message or give us a pat lesson in human relations. Though the poem presents the speaker's attitude more sympathetically than the neighbor's, it does not offer this as the total meaning. Frost's intent is to portray a problem and explore the many different and paradoxical issues it involves. He pictures it within an incident from rural life, and in order to reveal its complex nature he develops it through the conflict of two opposed points of view. The clash between the speaker and his neighbor lays bare the issue, which within their world is the simple matter of whether or not it is worthwhile to maintain the unnecessary wall in defiance of nature's persistent attempt to tear it down. But one cannot avoid looking at this problem in other contexts of experience. The wall becomes the symbol for all kinds of man-made barriers. The two views of it represent general attitudes towards life—the one, a surrender to the natural forces which draw human beings together, the other, the conservatism which persists in keeping up the distinctions separating them.

It is tempting to make the symbolic meaning more specific, and there has in fact been a good deal of speculation about just what the wall represents. Does it signify class divisions, the barriers of racial prejudice, the misunderstanding between nations, or differences of religion? Similarly, the opposed opinions of the speaker and the old farmer seem to invite a comparison with political, philosophical, and ethical positions. One might see the poem as a contrast between the liberal and the conservative, the instinctualist and the rationalist, the man of charity and the man of justice. However, common sense tells us that the search for a single set of symbolic referents is futile. The evidence is lacking, and what is more important, such interpretation cannot account for the broad range of symbolic meaning which gives the poem its beauty and interest.

At the same time it would be equally foolish to pretend that the poem is just about the problem of mending a pasture wall. The interpretations suggested above should not be dismissed too scornfully, for while none taken by itself is adequate, all are within the scope of the poem's meaning. That the symbolism of "Mending Wall" is general does not mean that it is indefinite. . . . Frost has exactly defined the nature of the problem he portrays, so that it represents, not vague classes of experience, but only other problems of the same kind. Though one may see in "Mending Wall" allusions to specific things outside the poem, even reminiscences of one's own past experience, their meanings will always have a certain fundamental similarity.

The comparison made earlier between Frost's mode of reference and the landscape vista indicates the kind of symbolism most characteristic of his work. Just as the vista delimits the observer's vision, Frost's symbols control the direction of the reader's thought; and although the path of reference may contain specific referents as the vista does objects, these are less interesting in themselves than the total view with its depth and the sense it creates of innumerable remote things related to the viewer's point of vantage. This conception should be helpful to the interpretation of Frost's poems. For one thing, it should save readers from the despairing view that, because his symbolic references are not specific, his poems lack any symbolic import and are to be taken merely as descriptions of particular places and personal experiences. Then, too, it should serve as a guard against the opposite absurdity, that of reading Frost's poems as if they were cryptograms in which every image has some set equivalent. By thinking of Frost's symbolic reference as a vista rather than an arrow moving from image to referent, one can recognize specific references and yet see them in their proper perspective as particular meanings within the scope of a more general meaning. In "Mending Wall," for example, the wall does suggest other kinds of barriers, the divisions between nations, classes, economic, racial, and religious groups and the like, but no one of these or combination of them all exhausts the symbol's meaning. Nevertheless they fall within the range of reference; to recognize their relevance is not to "read into" the poem, but to discover some small portion of what is actually there.

"OUT, OUT"

This view should demonstrate the need to scrutinize the symbolism of Frost's poetry. Even when the poet seems most determined to do no more than describe a scene or episode, his imagery has a significance which extends outward to range upon range of meaning. In "'Out, Out—,'" for example, he tells the story of how a boy loses his hand by accident while cutting wood at a buzz saw and dies only a few hours after. The effect of pathos is so intense that one may at first suppose that this constitutes the poem's main value. But sad events do not in themselves create moving poetry. Though Frost may seem only to describe, actually he has so managed his description that the boy's story symbolizes realities present everywhere in the human situation. The key to the poem's meaning is to be found in the fact that the loss of the hand causes almost immediate death:

> But the hand!
> The boy's first outcry was a rueful laugh,
> As he swung toward them holding up the hand
> Half in appeal, but half as if to keep
> The life from spilling. Then the boy saw all—
> Since he was old enough to know, big boy
> Doing a man's work, though a child at heart—
> He saw all spoiled.

Ordinarily an accident of this sort would not be mortal, especially when, as in this case, modern medical attention is within reach. "The doctor put him in the dark of ether," and there is no *physical* reason why he should not have recovered. His death is caused, rather, by his recognition of what the loss of a hand signifies in terms of his life: "the boy saw all—. . . He saw all spoiled." At the end

They listened at his heart.
Little—less—nothing!—and that ended it.
No more to build on there.

The "all" that the boy sees is the complete and irretrievable ruin of his life. Any merely medical explanation of his death is irrelevant. He does not die of shock or a too intense sorrow but of his realization of the truth. It cannot be a matter of enduring great pain for a time or of learning to get along as a cripple. There is no choice; he *must* die, and the reader will understand the poem to the extent that he sees why this is so.

All is spoiled because of the very nature of the world in which the boy lives. The long opening description has the important function of defining this world. It is, of course, the rural world, the scene of the accident being the farmyard where the boy, along with others, is cutting firewood. Frost pictures the setting as a sort of rustic amphitheatre with the snarling saw at its center and, extending away in the distance,

Five mountain ranges one behind the other
Under the sunset far into Vermont.

One should also note that the boy is working, not just playing at work as children elsewhere might, and that the work is expected of him. This emphasizes the fact that in his world a man's livelihood, even at an early age, depends upon hard physical labor. For him, then, the loss of the hand means not only a painful abnormality, but perhaps even the loss of his ability to survive.... In every context the hand is associated with power and creativity; in the boy's world, however, it is not just a symbol of these things, it is quite literally the instrument. The boy sees that in losing his hand he has lost the possibility of ever becoming fully a man, not only in the sense of being masculine, but in the sense of achieving the completeness of his nature. The poem implies that anything less than this completeness involves such a maiming that the individual, in an essential way, dies.

Some readers may prefer to view the poem simply as an episode illustrating the way in which horror bursts through the peaceful and familiar surface of life. Certainly, the boy's first reaction is one of surprise, rather than pain. Yet his death is the ultimate fact, and this is defined by his recognition of what the accident means. We can, I think, avoid "reading into" the poem by keeping in mind the fact that the boy's understanding is not a reasoned one, but comes in a flash of intuition. It is, one might say, a complete realization. And its completeness emphasizes the nature of the pastoral world: one gets the impression that only in such a world is the boy's intuitive recognition possible.

The title, of course, is taken from Macbeth's soliloquy upon learning of his wife's suicide, and there is some value in comparing the view of death presented in the poem with Macbeth's. As everyone will remember, the soliloquy describes life as meaningless, "a tale / Told by an idiot, full of sound and fury, / signifying nothing." Macbeth, because he refuses to recognize that guilt has caused his wife's death, as it will soon cause his own, cannot see the pattern which makes sense of events. Hence for him death also becomes

A POET OF RURAL SPIRIT

This piece ran within Robert Frost's obituary in the New York Times. *In it, author Thomas Lask praised Frost's ability to span urbanity to country life.*

Frost valued impulse over reason, transcendental truth over logic. But he did not entirely trust the impulses of other men —especially in a crowd. In "A Considerable Speck" he wrote:

> I have none of the tender-than-thou
> Collectivistic regimenting love
> With which the modern world is being swept.

In like spirit he turned his back on the city with its industrialization and its mass man. "I have outwalked the furthest city lights," he boasted proudly. In one of his most sharply written works, "Departmental," amusing in tone though not in intent, he excoriates the bureaucratic regimentation that has invaded and dogs our lives. In one poem he more than suggests that he has found more mind in a miniscule midge than in some of his contemporaries.

Yet it is precisely this stance, this point of view that was the source of his popularity. Frost spoke to a generation that had long left the farm, to a people who clustered increasingly around large cities, who more and more in homes and at their work accepted the mechanization of existence. But they kept brighter vision of rural life; they hankered for what they believed were the simplicities and virtues of country living. It is a vision that has one of the strongest holds on the imagination and fancy of the urban American. It goes back to some Adamic dream—to a Garden of Eden before the fall.

Thomas Lask, "A Poet of Rural Spirit," *New York Times*, January 30, 1963.

meaningless, a trifling occurrence, like the going out of a candle. Yet despite his professed indifference to death Macbeth clings to his faith in the witches' prophecies and fights on, even when all hope is lost. The boy seems to accept death with the same resignation as that expressed in Macbeth's lines, and in some ways the poem reflects the meaninglessness Macbeth describes. True, the loss of the hand is purely accidental; there is no particular reason in nature why it had to happen. But the ironic contrast between the boy's story and the soliloquy is more important than their similarity. For the boy, unlike Macbeth, "sees all," and he therefore does not struggle to live. Furthermore, his death is meaningful, since it defines his life. Both the boy and the reader see why it must be, whereas Macbeth cannot see the significance of death.

The comparison Frost invites us to make between the boy's story and Macbeth's illustrates the way the poem implies a commentary upon life as it is lived in areas far beyond the boy's humble world. Macbeth, after all, belongs to a world of heroic action and high politics, and the fact that he appears to be less wise than the boy shows us how the poet uses the contrast of pastoral to measure this exalted sphere by the standards of the simple scene he describes. The same process of measurement can be applied to other areas of meaning. For example, the poem leads one to raise the question as to whether life in modern urban society is not inferior to that of the boy's world. In the city, an injury such as the boy suffers would be curable and the victim would go on living, but that is so because the city represents a way of life in which man's physical being is not in such complete harmony with other aspects of his nature. The boy's death symbolizes not only a superior wisdom but a superior kind of existence, one in which there is a perfect coherence and order. The mind and body are unified, man's thought is manifested in physical action, and as we see in Frost's description of the sawdust—"Sweet-scented stuff when the breeze drew across it"—pleasure springs from natural, everyday things. The order and coherence make experience understandable, not only to the boy, who recognizes the truth so fully, but to the speaker, whose tone implies a clear grasp of the tragedy, and to those close to the boy: "And they, since they / Were not the one dead, turned to their affairs." This is not indifference, but a frank acceptance of reality, such an acceptance as would only be possible in a world so perfectly coherent that the truth is plain.

However, the poem also reveals the limitations of the boy's world and makes us aware of the ways in which the great world is superior. The death, after all, is a bitter thing; there is much to be said for a world in which one can survive an accident such as the boy's. Ironically, it is the very advantages of the rural world that make it, in other ways, inferior: the boy's conception of life is such that any impairment is fatal; and the rural world is so perfectly organized that any disruption of the natural order may lead to catastrophe.

So far I have stressed the differences the poem implies between the rural world and other levels of being, but here, as elsewhere in pastoral, the similarities are at least as important. The saw and the amputated hand are both richly symbolic. The saw, while only a machine, seems almost to possess a will and feelings of its own. It "snarled" as it cut the wood, and at the moment of the accident "Leaped out at the boy's hand, or seemed to leap." Yet its sinister aspect results from its lack of intent or feeling; it is dangerous because it is merely mechanical. The contrast between the machine and human nature is central. The boy loses his hand for the very reason that he has emotions, desires, and purposes beyond the saw's simple function of cutting wood. He is hurt because he turns away happily when he hears it is time for supper. The saw may have cut the hand "As if to prove saws knew what supper meant," but, of course, it didn't know or care. The hand, as I have said, suggests all man's faculties of strength and creativity; the saw comes to stand for all the mechanisms by means of which he works, from the simplest farm implement to the most complex economic institutions. Frost's story, then, deals with a good deal more than the boy's personal misfortune. It symbolizes a tragic aspect of the human situation: the fact that man's economic means, for the very reason that they are mechanical in nature, can destroy him. The death may not always be a physical one, as in the boy's case, but a destruction of man's essential humanity.

Frightening Encounters with Nature

Judith Oster

Judith Oster, in this excerpt from her book, *Toward Robert Frost: The Reader and the Poet*, discusses the poems "Stopping by Woods" and "Desert Places." Oster emphasizes Frost's use of whiteness and blankness to suggest loneliness and how they seem to scare the reader—and the poet.

Even if we had never read any Frost poems of leaves calling a person to join them in flight, or threatening him, or trying to carry him deathward, never seen trees as representing one's darkness of mood, or woods as frightening or attractive, we would find in "Stopping by Woods on a Snowy Evening" the basic conflict between attraction toward these woods and conscious resistance to that attraction—to use the verbs of the poem—between stopping and going:

Whose woods these are I think I know.
His house is in the village though;
He will not see me stopping here
To watch his woods fill up with snow.

My little horse must think it queer
To stop without a farmhouse near
Between the woods and frozen lake
The darkest evening of the year.

He gives his harness bells a shake
To ask if there is some mistake.
The only other sound's the sweep
Of easy wind and downy flake.

The woods are lovely, dark and deep,
But I have promises to keep,
And miles to go before I sleep,
And miles to go before I sleep.

The speaker of this poem is recounting a particular incident that takes place at a clearly specified woods on a clearly specified evening. Yet the title of the poem refuses specificity and concreteness. "Stopping by Woods (with no article, no noun marker) on *a* Snowy Evening" generalizes the experience to imply that this is not only one man's particular and peculiar experience: this is the way it is when one stops by woods on a snowy evening. This is the nature of stopping at such a place in such circumstances. Snowy woods can *have* this effect.

What, exactly, is the effect? So moved is the traveler by the sight of woods filling up with snow that he stops. Conscious first of all of the owner whose house is in the village, safely and sensibly away from snowy woods, he seems to need to assure himself that the owner will not see him stopping there. For one thing, he would presumably prefer that the owner not see him trespassing; but for another, sensitive as he is to the mentality of the horse, he would probably feel foolish were he seen by another man—especially by a man whose house is in the village. It would be difficult to explain why he is stopping on such a night at such a place. This need not to be seen adds to the feeling of isolation that the poem has already provided in showing the man's aloneness. Not only does he happen to be the only person on the scene, but he is doing what someone more sensible would not do, or what a less sensitive person would not do—stop at the worst possible time simply because a scene is so attractive. In this sense the traveler welcomes his solitude, luxuriates in an experience he need not share or explain.

The judgment of "queerness" is his own, as he projects it onto his horse, and this further isolates him. Not only might he be judged by the man in the village, but even his horse thinks he is queer. Robert Penn Warren makes a very apt distinction between man, who is capable of dreaming and appreciating, and the horse, who is not. There is, however, another set of contrasts. The man in the village would judge him based on standards of sensible if unimaginative practicality. This traveler, though, chooses, for the moment at least, the world of nature, of snowy woods as opposed to the village. Why then this imagined judgment on the part of an animal? An animal, a creature of no imagination, will do what is instinctive for its safety. Wanting to get home, out of the snow, dictates the shake of the reins. A deer would have run into the woods. This horse, however, has his place of rest in a barn. Tamed, domesticated, this animal stands somewhere between woods and civilization. And the man, between horse and woods, stands there as well. Human though he may be, he is drawn toward those woods, just as that horse, animal though he is, is drawn home to the barn.

The woods are dark and deep. Not frightening, this dark, not nightmarish, this unknown, but lovely, attractive even in the depth of its darkness, perhaps because of it. Because this lovely darkness is so quickly counteracted by "promises," it has been easy to see the lure of this darkness as the lure of whatever dark and lovely thing stands in opposition to promises, with its overtones of obligation (perhaps to society, family, self, a higher power, or moral code) and which requires something as strong and binding as "promises" to break the spell and call the traveler back to the road.

We could name many things, but they would probably all have in common some version of freedom from that which binds us to promises, to obligation or duty, to a sense of right and wrong—a freedom from awareness of the boundary between woods and road, or of any boundaries at all. Fundamental to all aspects of the contrary pulls, even the literal one of going as opposed to stopping, is the sense of responsibility that obtrudes itself at the end, probably winning over the impulse to irresponsibility, or perhaps the more specific irresponsible impulse. . . .

FROST'S WILDNESS

Wildness stands in opposition to cultivation and tameness, to restraint, order, and predictability, it also stands in opposition to the boundaries, duties, and rules that are represented by "promises." We have seen that the wildness in Frost seems to have frightened him on occasion. He had also spoken of "wildness" in poetry in "The Figure a Poem Makes," opposing it to the steadiness that comes from theme and subject: "to have . . . wildness pure, to be wild with nothing to be wild about . . . [is] giving way to undirected associations." At a later date Frost related this passage to his own nature: "I lead a life estranged from myself. . . . I am very wild at heart sometimes. Not at all confused. Just wild—wild. Couldn't you read it between the lines in my Preface nay and in the lines?". . .

In another reference to wildness and its effect on sanity, . . . Frost wrote that "we can make raids and excursions into the wild, but it has to be from well kept strongholds.". . .

Ease and relaxation are among the most remarkable features of this poem. Like those snowy woods, the poem can lull us into an unaware acceptance only of its loveliness. The linked rhyme scheme draws us on from one stanza to the next, culminating in the repetend this scheme demanded, the perfect repetition that simultaneously soothes, concludes, and opens up further extensions of meaning. The rhyme contributes to the lulling effect, for this poem is a rare example in Frost of near-complete regularity—strict iambics with no caesuras, no pauses. The only exception occurs in the last stanza where we pause slightly at the comma after "lovely," as if we are being prepared for the slight jolt of "promises"—that decisive word on which the poem turns, and the man turns. One can read the line with metric perfection, but to do so is to violate what Frost considers so important: the tones of real speech. This line is an excellent illustration of "the possibility for tune from the dramatic tones of meaning struck across the rigidity of limited meter," and the tension between the two reflects perfectly the tension that "promises" exerts on the man and on the experience.

Were it not for the turn because of "promises," we too might forget what snow is associated with in other poems, and how cold it is in reality, for we are told nothing of this. Besides the harness bells, "the only other sound's the sweep of easy wind and downy flake." The softness of the repeated "s" and "n" sounds adds to the "ease" of the wind, the softness of the snowflakes. They are downy, like a bed, and the man is thinking of sleep. The temptation to give in is not only to give in to relaxation of rules—to abandon—it is to give in to rest, to cessation, to stopping, and surely by now the snow has obscured the clear lines that divide road from woods.

When asked in a television interview what he thought of this poem's having been interpreted as a suicide poem, Frost replied, "That's terrible, isn't it?" The question may have referred to [John] Ciardi's article, which was widely circulated and very well known. Ciardi called it unmistakably a "death wish," a statement he has since wisely revised to a question. [Frost biographer Lawrance] Thompson, however, only suggested that Ciardi recognize that the death wish is resisted, a rather obvious point. Indeed, the biography shows a great deal of evidence that Frost toyed with the notion of suicide throughout his life, perhaps most often during the Derry years. There *was* a frozen pond he used to pass coming from the village, and he did tell Elizabeth Sergeant of a "black 'tarn'... (for convenient suicide), and what a pang it cost the poet not to have chosen it." Even more telling are two poems he chose never to publish: "Despair" is about suicide by drowning—a poem he knew by heart in his old age, the other is "To Prayer I Go," about which he wrote to Louis Untermeyer at one time: "That is my last, my ultimate vileness, that I cannot make up my mind to go now where I must go sooner or later. I am afraid." And at another time: "I decided to keep the matter private and out of my new book. It could easily be made too much of. I can't myself say how serious the crisis was and how near I came to giving in." Whether the reference in these letters is to prayer or to death seems almost irrelevant, for the two go together in the third and final version of the poem, a going down to a crucified and penitential death in prayer.

So much for expecting Frost to admit on television that "Stopping by Woods" is a "suicide poem." We must ultimately judge by returning to the poem, where once again we wonder how much can be loaded onto a delicate lyric. Of course, as we have noted elsewhere, Frost has us, the readers, both ways: if we see nothing but snowy woods, we have been lulled by it; if we see every possibility, we have been lured by it into weighting it with possibly unwarranted meanings, or into exposing ourselves in our readings. It is precisely here that we see once again the artistry of Frost; while remaining the simple and beautiful lyric poem that it is, *it* opens itself to extensions of meaning that are possible—but only possible. That dark, deep woods can be dangerously lovely, dangerously wild; that death is the ultimate relaxation, the ultimate destination, and the ultimate escape from the world everyone knows. Whether these are the subjects of the poem no one knows. We have no right to say that this poem is about suicide, or moral or psychic wildness; only that it *might* be. We *can* say that it is about resisting an attractive invitation extended by the beauty of nature, an invitation to forget promises.

In the same way we can only conjecture whether the speaker feels any kind of identity with those woods, whether the pull they exert on him to enter corresponds with something within him that demands withdrawal into self and away from promises. In "Desert Places," however, the traveler explicitly relates the snowy scene to himself.

"DESERT PLACES": LONELINESS AND FEAR

Snow falling and night falling fast, oh, fast
In a field I looked into going past,
And the ground almost covered smooth in snow,
But a few weeds and stubble showing last.

The woods around it have it—it is theirs.
All animals are smothered in their lairs.
I am too absent-spirited to count;
The loneliness includes me unawares.

And lonely as it is that loneliness
Will be more lonely ere it will be less—
A blanker whiteness of benighted snow
With no expression, nothing to express.

They cannot scare me with their empty spaces
Between stars—on stars where no human race is.
I have it in me so much nearer home
To scare myself with my own desert places.

This later poem makes a fitting companion piece to "Stopping by Woods." Even the rhyme scheme (aaba) is the same, although in this poem, the poet has not chosen to commit himself to the greater difficulty of linking his stanzas by means of rhyme. This speaker too is traveling through falling snow at nightfall. The woods are present in this poem as well, though we are more conscious of their darkness in "Stopping by Woods" and more conscious of whiteness here. While the opening line sounds soothing with its repetition of "s," and "f," and "o," we know as early as the second line that this speaker does not stop, even for a moment—the fields he describes are those he is "going past." What is not presented as frightening in "Stopping by Woods" is frightening in this poem. Nothing here makes one feel that the speaker finds this snowfall attractive, nothing draws him in, for this snowfall does not present a relaxing oblivion; it presents a concrete blankness. Because it is with blankness that he identifies, it presents no escape, only a reminder of self, a self that is not a welcome haven or wellspring. Withdrawal would not be "strategic" and self-preserving. It would be facing a desert.

The open space is surrounded by woods that "have it." They claim it, and the speaker willingly relegates it to them—willing not because of a decision he has struggled to make, but because he is too apathetic, "too absent-spirited to count." The structural ambiguity in this line and its seeming carelessness emphasize his absent-spiritedness, his apathy. We cannot be sure whether "count" is being used in its active sense (to count, to tell what is happening, to reckon up woods, animals and fields) or in its passive sense (to be counted, to count to anything or anyone else). The following line is also enriched by its apparently careless use of "unawares," which could modify "loneliness" or could modify "me." Again, the ambiguous use of the word illustrates that very unawareness, that carelessness that causes us to associate absent-spiritedness with absent-mindedness.

In the third stanza loneliness is in apposition to snow, and just as the snow will cover more and more, will leave nothing uncovered to relieve its smooth unbroken whiteness, so the loneliness will become still more lonely and unrelieved. That same whiteness—snow or loneliness—is what makes desert of a field, helps the woods to "have" the fields in that it obliterates clear boundaries between field and woods, raising, as it does in "Stopping by Woods," the dangerous prospect of boundarilessness. Even when the journey is into one's *own* desert places, one's humanity or identity is threatened, and loneliness, the apposition suggests, can do this too. What terrifies him so much, however, is not the fact that he is alone, without other people, but that alone with himself he may find nothing—no one and nothing within. Whereas "Stopping by Woods" presented an invitation to the solitude and inertia of snow, this poem presents the attendant fear that once giving in to the self, or going into the self, he will find that the journey has been for nothing. That there is nothing but loneliness, blankness, and absent-spiritedness in the sense of absence of spirit.

The "nothingness" that Frost fears is not the metaphysical void, it is the void he fears in himself. In relating this personal void to the spaces between stars, he suggests that a personal void can have—or seem to have—cosmic proportions, that it can seem at *least* as important, as vast and as frightening, as anything "out there." This speaker fears the void, but . . . he is capable of beholding what is not there. He is not a man of snow because he has enough feeling to be afraid. His is not yet a "mind of winter," for he can still think about having one, fear that he might discover it if he explores inside himself. He has it "in him"—again, as in "Spring Pools"—the threatening potential of what lies within. The man with the "mind of winter" does not think, but to [poet Wallace] Stevens there are two kinds of nothingness—"the nothing that is" and "nothing," which is the absence of something. The greater lack is the latter—the absence of imagination in the man who "beholds nothing that is not there." In "Desert Places" the speaker fears blankness "with no expression, nothing to express." There is a difference between "nothing to express" and an expression of nothingness, as Stevens has shown us. The fear in the poem is of the former, but the act of the poem is the latter.

For the poet there is an additional terror in identifying his own "desert places" with the blank landscape: it is a "whiteness . . . with no expression, nothing to express." If there is nothing there, nothing showing or growing, if there is no spirit, what will he have to say? This fear of nothing to say was a constant one to Frost. To Untermeyer he once confided "a very damaging secret. . . . The poet in me died nearly ten years ago. . . . The calf I was in the nineties I merely take to market. . . . Take care that you don't get your mouth set to declare the other two [books] a falling off of power, for that is what they can't be. . . . As you look back don't you see how a lot of things I have said begin to take meaning from this? . . . I tell you, Louis, it's all over at thirty. . . . Anyway that was the way I thought I might feel. And I took measures accordingly. . . . I have myself all in a strong box." Having nothing more to say was what he assumed lay behind Hemingway's decision to commit suicide—a motive and a decision Frost defended.

Even worse than having nothing to say, perhaps, is emotional poverty—feeling used up, both by the pain of events in life and by the demands of his art. He once wrote: "[poets] are so much less sensitive from having overused their sensibilities. Men who have to feel for a living would unavoidably become altogether unfeeling except professionally." Whatever the basis, the poem ends with the fear of one's own emptiness, one's own nothingness. To traverse these spaces inside the self is to traverse the barren.

At the same time, though, and characteristically, the fear is expressed with a kind of bravado: "they can't scare *me!*" the comparison between the interstellar spaces and his own desert places also serves to aggrandize the speaker and the importance of his personal desert. Then, also characteristically, Frost undercuts both the bravado and the self-importance, mainly by means of metrics. Where the speaker tries so hard to show strength the lines end weakly: they are the only feminine rhymes in the poem; the three rhyming lines of the last stanza all have an added, unstressed eleventh syllable: /əz/. The effect in lines 13 and 14 is to undercut the tone of confidence. By the last line, where bravado gives in to fear, the unstressed ending reinforces the fear by sounding weak in the face of what is feared. The ´ ˘ rhyme concluding the poem also works against a feeling of closure and resolution.

While the whole final stanza has its metrical bumps, line 14 jolts us the most and alerts us to other tensions with and within that line. For example, whereas "spaces" and "places" are both noun objects of prepositions, rhyming what is also structurally parallel, "race is," as a noun subject and verb, seems out of kilter with the other two. To focus more closely, though, on these words is to notice the possible pun "where no human races" and the tensions *that* produces between the two possible meanings: in one sense, the contrast between a place where people do not race—no rushing, no competition—and a world where the need to go forward quickly and competitively obtains even in one's private desert. Following on this contrast is another: the active verb of one reading—"races"—contrasts with the static "is" of the other, which creates further tensions. Grammatically, the two would be awkward together, as we do not coordinate an active verb with a stative one. Semantically, the difference is related to two conflicting needs: going, doing, rushing to compete and simply being. Such stasis, though, is located where there is no human life. . . . Seen this way, the poem presents another version of the conflict between going and stopping, motion and stasis. While in this poem the outward action is not stopping but going *past* the field (he races?), what inner desert it represents, of course, goes with him, and, as "Stopping by Woods" reminds us, we must go—move, do—if we are to be.

Nature, Tragedy, and the Question of Evil

Robert M. Rechnitz

Robert M. Rechnitz, a Frost scholar and essayist, examines Frost's use of nature in his poems and compares it to William Shakespeare's use of dramatic characters. Rechnitz contends, however, that it would be wrong to see nature as either all good or all evil; since it reflects humanity, nature is almost always a mixture of both.

In what is perhaps the most jubilant of essays ever written about Robert Frost, Randall Jarrell speaks of the regrettable and inescapable dilemma attendant upon the creation of art in the present century. Man's expanding awareness of himself and his universe has resulted in a discontinuity of the poetic imagination. Thus, of Frost's achievements Jarrell remarks: "If we compare this wisdom with, say, that of Goethe, we are saddened and frightened at how much the poet's scope has narrowed, at how difficult and partial and idiosyncratic the application of his intelligence has become, at what terrible sacrifices he has had to make in order to avoid making others still more terrible."

A TRAGIC VISION WITHOUT CONVENTIONAL TRAGIC HEROES

Coming at once to Frost's greatest sacrifice, we note the absence in his dramatic family of an Antony, a Hamlet, a Macbeth. In their stead we find a Hill Wife, a Servant to Servants, an Old Man. History is responsible for the discovery of value in such lives.

Though there are no tragic heroes in his work, Frost does maintain a tragic vision of the universe, a tragic vision resistant to concise definition, since it exists as an attitude rather than as a concept. The universe remains vast and incomprehensible except for those vague promptings of the

Reprinted from Robert M. Rechnitz, "The Tragic Vision of Robert Frost," in *Frost: Centennial Essays*, compiled by the Committee on the Frost Centennial of the University of Southern Mississippi (Jackson: University Press of Mississippi, 1974–78), by permission of the publisher.

sensibility which defy articulation, but which imply

That though there is no fixed line between wrong and right,
There are roughly zones whose laws must be obeyed.

Nature's laws are seen but darkly. "Something there is that doesn't love a wall," but the something is never defined. One misreads the poem, however, if he misses Frost's imputation of a moral regard in nature's fretful anarchy. If morality within anarchy is dismissed as a meaningless paradox, the richness of a tragic universe will not be perceived.

The idea of the ultimate power as a kind of fate receives the greater part of Robert Frost's attention. Any progression of thought on this subject must be ours, for it is almost certain that Frost holds these various attitudes simultaneously. Yet in one poem the poet reveals himself in the act of revising his thoughts. "The Stars" are regarded first as being a sympathetic audience attending us "As if with keenness for our fate," but in the last stanza Frost shifts his ground:

And yet with neither love nor hate
Those stars like some snow-white
Minerva's snow-white marble eyes
Without the gift of sight.

It is this latter attitude toward nature that is on the one hand so representative of our time and on the other so unsympathetic to the artistic imagination that Frost seldom adopts it; perhaps this is one occasion that Mr. Jarrell has in mind when he speaks of the modern poet's partial and idiosyncratic application of his intellect. Perhaps such a view of nature appeals most to Frost's intellect, but it must soon be abandoned because of its sterility.

ALMIGHTY NATURE

Besides, nature is *not* so aloof. If we turn our backs, nature steals a pace forward. With "The Wood-Pile," Frost amplifies the idea of nature's unremitting warfare upon mankind. The poem achieves its end by contrasting the puniness and specificity of man with the featureless ambiance of nature. As the poem opens, the narrator is absorbed in his playful exchange with the little bird; both man and bird are individuals—that is the important thing—and they are communicating with each other in a pleasant, ordinary way, the very normalcy of which sustains them both. It is the presence of the bird that makes the wilderness bearable, that holds it back and gives it form. With the discovery of the woodpile, a sudden change occurs. The bird departs and nature closes in. The woodpile is gray; the world itself turns gray as if enshrouded in fog. The poet confronts chaos, utter formlessness—void. And this void is busily reclaiming that to which man has given shape.

The poem amounts to a synthesis of the remote unconcern of nature and of nature's hostility. Like the pan of dough which fills in the dimples we poke in it, nature slowly sloughs off our efforts to mold it. It is nature's inertia which balks us; its entropy defies man, the champion of progress. It is the poet in Frost that sees this inertia as hostility; it is the twentieth century in him which sees it as mere indifference.

IS NATURE EVIL? IS IT LIKE US?

The poet's problem remains: he must search for means to dramatize the hostility or indifference. In "The Most of It," nature answers man's cry of loneliness and desire for "counter-love, original response" by sending him a wild beast.

> As the great buck it powerfully appeared,
> Pushing the crumpled water up ahead,
> And landed pouring like a waterfall,
> And stumbled through the rocks with horny tread,
> And forced the underbrush—and that was all.

The repeated use, four times in three lines, of "and" establishes the lack of causality, the absence of meaning. Man constitutes his world in part by a constant attempt to discover cause and effect, and he is brought up short when he cannot do so. Nature at odd moments—this poem visualizes one of them—is easily capable of working not from causality but from mere sequence.

Still, we cannot infer that nature is evil or that an ultimate power working behind and through nature is evil. We have discovered inertia and simple sequence, but nothing more than that; and neither of these can be termed evil except insofar as they subvert man's will to order. The universe may be enigmatic, but that is not to say it is malign.

In a deceptive little poem, "Spring Pools," Frost records another sequence, this time one in which man is little concerned. The poem can easily be dismissed as a simple pastoral. The tone is tranquil throughout, even the last stanza of the admonition. But though the poem deals with spring pools and flowers, with trees and summer foliage, the implication is sinister: the process of life is predatory. Birth is achieved at the expense of life. The trees draw their life-blood vampire-like from the pools, the pools from the winter snow, and so on, each element in nature drawing from each to an extent guaranteed to elate the most fervent Darwinian. Of course, only the cheapest sort of sentimentality would label natural rapacity as evil; but carried a step further, this implication takes on all the metaphysical horror of a poem like "Design." It would be pretentious to attempt to add anything to Randall Jarrell's commentary on the poem, but Reginald L. Cook offers a remark which contributes to my thesis: Frost's "conjectural inquiry in 'Design' not only implies a subtle but a malefic force at work. And if design operates on the lower level in nature—if it is in the ruck of little things—then, by extension, it must also operate generally in the human sphere of activity since man cannot be separated from the complex, interrelated destiny of the natural universe." Man cannot be separated from the universe around him, and this is, of course, the justification for any poet's concern with nature. There is a correspondence, however tenuous, which the poet senses when his heart vibrates in sympathy with a windhover or lark. Furthermore, we sympathize with the fat, dimpled spider, and with all the other carnivores which inhabit the earth and whose habits we recognize in our own.

CHAPTER 3

Close Reading of Selected Frost Poems

READINGS ON
ROBERT FROST

Rhyme and Symbol in "Stopping by Woods"

John Ciardi

John Ciardi, who has written extensively about poetry in general and Robert Frost in particular, examines the symbols and the conclusion of "Stopping by Woods on a Snowy Evening." He suggests that the question we should ask of this popular poem is not "what does it mean" but rather "how does it mean?"

To read any one poem carefully is the ideal preparation for reading another. Only a poem can illustrate how poetry works. . . .

What happens in it?—which is to say, not *what* does it mean, but *how* does it mean? How does it go about being a human reenactment of a human experience? The author—perhaps the thousandth reader would need to be told—is Robert Frost.

Even the TV audience can see that this poem begins as a seemingly-simple narration of a seemingly-simple incident but ends by suggesting meanings far beyond anything specifically referred to in the narrative. And even readers with only the most casual interest in poetry might be made to note the additional fact that, though the poem suggests those larger meanings, it is very careful never to abandon its pretense to being simple narration. There is duplicity at work. The poet pretends to be talking about one thing, and all the while he is talking about many others.

Many readers are forever unable to accept the poet's essential duplicity. It is almost safe to say that a poem is never about what it seems to be about. As much could be said of the proverb. The bird in the hand, the rolling stone, the stitch in time never (except by an artful double-deception) intend any sort of statement about birds, stones, or sewing. The incident

Abridged from John Ciardi, "Robert Frost: The Way to the Poem," *Saturday Review*, April 12, 1958. Reprinted by permission of Myra Ciardi.

of this poem, one must conclude, is at root a metaphor. . . .

There is nothing wrong-in-itself with a tacked-on moral. Frost, in fact, makes excellent use of the device at times. In this poem, however, Frost is careful to let the whatever-the-moral-is grow out of the poem itself. When the action ends the poem ends. There is no epilogue and no explanation. Everything pretends to be about the narrated incident. And that pretense sets the basic tone of the poem's performance of itself.

THREE SCENES

The dramatic force of that performance is best observable, I believe, as a progression in three scenes.

In scene one, which coincides with stanza one, a man—a New England man—is driving his sleigh somewhere at night. It is snowing, and as the man passes a dark patch of woods he stops to watch the snow descend into the darkness. We know, moreover, that the man is familiar with these parts (he knows who owns the woods and where the owner lives), and we know that no one has seen him stop. As scene one forms itself in the theatre of the mind's-eye, therefore, it serves to establish some as yet unspecified relation between the man and the woods.

It is necessary, however, to stop here for a long parenthesis: Even so simple an opening statement raises any number of questions. It is impossible to address all the questions that rise from the poem stanza by stanza, but two that arise from stanza one illustrate the sort of thing one might well ask of the poem detail by detail.

Why, for example, does the man not say what errand he is on? What is the force of leaving the errand generalized? He might just as well have told us that he was going to the general store, or returning from it with a jug of molasses he had promised to bring Aunt Harriet and two suits of long underwear he had promised to bring the hired man. Frost, moreover, can handle homely detail to great effect. He preferred to leave his motive generalized. Why?

And why, on the other hand, does he say so much about knowing the absent owner of the woods and where he lives? Is it simply that one set of details happened-in whereas another did not? To speak of things "happening-in" is to assault the integrity of a poem. Poetry cannot be discussed meaningfully unless one can assume that everything in the poem—

every last comma and variant spelling—is in it by the poet's specific act of choice. Only bad poets allow into their poems what is haphazard or cheaply chosen.

The errand, I will venture a bit brashly for lack of space, is left generalized in order the more aptly to suggest *any* errand in life and, therefore, life itself. The owner is there because he is one of the forces of the poem. Let it do to say that the force he represents is the village of mankind (that village at the edge of winter) from which the poet finds himself separated (has separated himself?) in his moment by the woods (and to which, he recalls finally, he has promises to keep). The owner is he-who-lives-in-his-village-house, thereby locked away from the poet's awareness of the-time-the-snow-tells as it engulfs and obliterates the world the village man allows himself to believe he "owns." Thus, the owner is a representative of an order of reality from which the poet has divided himself for the moment, though to a certain extent he ends by reuniting with it. Scene one, therefore, establishes not only a relation between the man and the woods, but the fact that the man's relation begins with his separation (though momentarily) from mankind.

End parenthesis one, begin parenthesis two.

Still considering the first scene as a kind of dramatic performance of forces, one must note that the poet has meticulously matched the simplicity of his language to the pretended simplicity of the narrative. Clearly, the man stopped because the beauty of the scene moved him, but he neither tells us that the scene is beautiful nor that he is moved. A bad writer, always ready to overdo, might have written: "The vastness gripped me, filling my spirit with the slow steady sinking of the snow's crystalline perfection into the glimmerless profundities of the hushed primeval wood." Frost's avoidance of such a spate illustrates two principles of good writing. The first, he has stated himself in "The Mowing": "Anything *more* than the truth would have seemed too weak" (italics mine). Understatement is one of the basic sources of power in English poetry. The second principle is to let the action speak for itself. A good novelist does not tell us that a given character is good or bad (at least not since the passing of the Dickens tradition): he shows us the character in action and then, watching him, we know. Poetry, too, has fictional obligations: even when the characters are ideas and metaphors rather than people, they must be *characterized in action.* A poem does not *talk about* ideas; it *enacts* them. The force of the poem's performance, in fact, is precisely to act out (and thereby to make us act out empathically, that is, *to feel out,* that is, *to identify with*) the speaker and why he stopped. The man is the principle actor in this little "drama of why" and in scene one he is the only character, though as noted, he is somehow related to the absent owner.

End second parenthesis.

SCENE TWO

In scene two (stanzas two and three) a *foil* is introduced. In fiction and drama, a foil is a character who "plays against" a more important character. By presenting a different point of view or an opposed set of motives, the foil moves the more important character to react in ways that might not have found expression without such opposition. The more important character is thus more fully revealed—to the reader and to himself. The foil here is the horse.

The horse forces the question. Why did the man stop? Until it occurs to him that his "little horse must think it queer" he had not asked himself for reasons. He had simply stopped. But the man finds himself faced with the question he imagines the horse to be asking: what *is* there to stop for out there in the cold, away from bin and stall (house and village and mankind?) and all that any self-respecting beast could value on such a night? In sensing that other view, the man is forced to examine his own more deeply.

In stanza two the question arises only as a feeling within the man. In stanza three, however (still scene two), the horse acts. He gives his harness bells a shake. "What's wrong?" he seems to say. "What are we waiting for?"

By now, obviously, the horse—without losing its identity as horse—has also become a symbol. A symbol is something that stands for something else. Whatever that something else may be, it certainly begins as that order of life that does not understand why a man stops in the wintry middle of nowhere to watch the snow come down. (Can one fail to sense by now that the dark and the snowfall symbolize a death-wish, however momentary, *i.e.,* that hunger for final rest and surrender that a man may feel, but not a beast?)

So by the end of scene two the performance has given dramatic force to three elements that work upon the man. There is his relation to the world of the owner. There is his relation to the brute world of the horse. And there is that third presence of the unownable world, the movement of the all-engulfing snow across all the orders of life, the man's, the owner's, and the horse's—with the difference that the man knows of that second dark-within-the-dark of which the horse cannot, and the owner will not, know.

The man ends scene two with all these forces working upon him simultaneously. He feels himself moved to a decision. And he feels a last call from the darkness: "the sweep/Of easy wind and downy flake." It would be so easy and so downy to go into the woods and let himself be covered over.

SCENE THREE

But scene three (stanza four) produces a fourth force. This fourth force can be given many names. It is certainly better, in fact, to give it many names than to attempt to limit it to one. It is social obligation, or personal commitment, or duty, or just the realization that a man cannot indulge a mood forever. All of these and more. But, finally, he has a simple decision to make. He may go into the woods and let the darkness and the snow swallow him from the world of beast and man. Or he must move on. And unless he is going to stop here forever, it is time to remember that he has a long way to go and that he had best be getting there. (So there is something to be said for the horse, too.)

Then and only then, his question driven more and more deeply into himself by these cross-forces, does the man venture a comment on what attracted him: "The woods are lovely, dark and deep." His mood lingers over the thought of that lovely dark-and-deep (as do the very syllables in which he phrases the thought), but the final decision is to put off the mood and move on. He has his man's way to go and his man's obligations to tend to before he can yield. He has miles to go before his sleep. He repeats that thought and the performance ends.

But why the repetition? The first time Frost says "And miles to go before I sleep," there can be little doubt that the primary meaning is: "I have a long way to go before I get to bed tonight." The second time he says it, however, "miles to go" and "sleep" are suddenly transformed into symbols. What are those "something-elses" the symbols stand for? Hundreds of people have tried to ask Mr. Frost that question and he has always turned it away. He has turned it away *be-*

cause he cannot answer it. He could answer some part of it. But some part is not enough.

For a symbol is like a rock dropped into a pool: it sends out ripples in all directions, and the ripples are in motion. Who can say where the last ripple disappears? One may have a sense that he knows the approximate center point of the ripples, the point at which the stone struck the water. Yet even then he has trouble marking it surely. How does one make a mark on water? Oh very well—the center point of that second "miles to go" is probably approximately in the neighborhood of being close to meaning, perhaps, "the road of life"; and the second "before I sleep" is maybe that close to meaning "before I take my final rest," the rest in darkness that seemed so temptingly dark-and-deep for the moment of the mood. But the ripples continue to move and the light to change on the water, and the longer one watches the more changes he sees. Such shifting-and-being-at-the-same-instant is of the very sparkle and life of poetry. One experiences it as one experiences life, for everytime he looks at an experience he sees something new, and he sees it change as he watches it. And that sense of continuity in fluidity is one of the primary kinds of knowledge, one of man's basic ways of knowing, and one that only the arts can teach, poetry foremost among them.

Frost himself certainly did not ask what that repeated last line meant. It came to him and he received it. He "felt right" about it. And what he "felt right" about was in no sense a "meaning" that, say, an essay could apprehend, but an act of experience that could be fully presented only by the dramatic enactment of forces which is the performance of the poem.

Now look at the poem in another way. Did Frost know what he was going to do when he began? Considering the poem simply as an act of skill, as a piece of juggling, one cannot fail to respond to the magnificent turn at the end where, with one flip, seven of the simplest words in the language suddenly dazzle full of never-ending waves of thought and feeling. Or, more precisely, of felt-thought. Certainly an equivalent stunt by a juggler—could there be an equivalent—would bring the house down. Was it to cap his performance with that grand stunt that Frost wrote the poem?

Far from it. The obvious fact is that *Frost could not have known he was going to write those lines until be wrote them.* Then a second fact must be registered: *he wrote them be-*

cause, for the fun of it, he had got himself into trouble.

Frost, like every good poet, began by playing a game with himself. The most usual way of writing a four line stanza with four feet to the line is to rhyme the third line with the first, and the fourth line with the second. Even that much rhyme is so difficult in English that many poets and almost all of the anonymous ballad makers do not bother to rhyme the first and third lines at all, settling for two rhymes in four lines as good enough. For English is a rhyme-poor language. In Italian and in French, for example, so many words end with the same sounds that rhyming is relatively easy—so easy that many modern French and Italian poets do not bother to rhyme at all. English, being a more agglomerate language, has far more final sounds, hence fewer of them rhyme. When an Italian poet writes a line ending with "vita" (life) he has literally hundreds of rhyme choices available. When an English poet writes "life" at the end of a line he can summon "strife, wife, knife, fife, rife," and then he is in trouble. Now "life-strife" and "life-rife" and "life-wife" seem to offer a combination of possible ideas that can be related by more than just the rhyme. Inevitably, therefore, the poets have had to work and rework these combinations until the sparkle has gone out of them. The reader is normally tired of such rhyme-led associations. When he encounters "life-strife" he is certainly entitled to suspect that the poet did not really want to say "strife"—that had there been in English such a word as, say, "hife," meaning "infinite peace and harmony," the poet would as gladly have used that word instead of "strife." Thus, the reader feels that the writing is haphazard, that the rhyme is making the poet say things he does not really feel, and which, therefore, the reader does not feel except as boredom. One likes to see the rhymes fall into place, but he must end with the belief that it is the poet who is deciding what is said and not the rhyme scheme that is forcing the saying.

So rhyme is a kind of game, and an especially difficult one in English. As in every game, the fun of the rhyme is to set one's difficulties high and then to meet them skillfully. As Frost himself once defined freedom, it consists of "moving easy in harness."

In "Stopping by Woods on a Snowy Evening" Frost took a long chance. He decided to rhyme not two lines in each stanza, but three. Not even Frost could have sustained that much rhyme in a long poem (as Dante, for example, with the advantage of writing in Italian, sustained triple rhyme for thousands of lines in "The Divine Comedy"). Frost would have known instantly, therefore, when he took the original chance, that he was going to write a short poem. He would have had that much foretaste of it.

So the first stanza emerged rhymed a-a-b-a. And with the sure sense that this was to be a short poem, Frost decided to take an additional chance and to redouble: in English three rhymes in four lines is more than enough; there is no need to rhyme the fourth line. For the fun of it, however, Frost set himself to pick up that loose rhyme and to weave it into the pattern, thereby accepting the all but impossible burden of quadruple rhyme.

The miracle is that it worked. Despite the enormous freight of rhyme, the poem not only came out as a neat pattern, but managed to do so with no sense of strain. Every word and every rhyme falls into place as naturally and as inevitably as if there were no rhyme restricting the poet's choices.

That ease-in-difficulty is certainly inseparable from the success of the poem's performance. One watches the skill-man juggle three balls, then four, then five, and every addition makes the trick more wonderful. But unless he makes the hard trick seem as easy as an easy trick, then all is lost.

The real point, however, is not only that Frost took on a hard rhyme-trick and made it seem easy. It is rather as if the juggler, carried away, had tossed up one more ball than he could really handle, and then amazed himself by actually handling it. So with the real triumph of this poem. Frost could not have known what a stunning effect his repetition of the last line was going to produce. He could not even know he was going to repeat the line. He simply found himself up against a difficulty he almost certainly had not fore-seen and he had to improvise to meet it. For in picking up the rhyme from the third line of stanza one and carrying it over into stanza two, he had created an endless chain-link form within which each stanza left a hook sticking out for the next stanza to hang on. So by stanza four, feeling the poem rounding to its end, Frost had to do something about that extra rhyme.

He might have tucked it back into a third line rhyming with the *know-though-snow* of stanza one. He could thus have rounded the poem out to the mathematical symmetry of using each rhyme four times. But though such a device might be defensible in theory, a rhyme repeated after eleven lines is so far from its original rhyme sound that its feeling as rhyme must certainly be lost And what good is theory if the reader is not moved by the writing?

It must have been in some such quandary that the final repetition suggested itself—a suggestion born of the very difficulties the poet had let himself in for. So there is that point beyond mere ease in handling a hard thing, the point at which the very difficulty offers the poet the opportunity to do better than he knew he could. What, aside from having that happen to oneself, could be more self-delighting than to participate in its happening by one's reader-identification with the poem?

And by now a further point will have suggested itself: that the human-insight of the poem and the technicalities of its poetic artifice are inseparable. Each feeds the other. That interplay is the poem's meaning, a matter not of WHAT DOES IT MEAN, for no one can ever say entirely what a good poem means, but of HOW DOES IT MEAN, a process one can come much closer to discussing.

There is a necessary epilogue. Mr. Frost has often discussed this poem on the platform, or more usually in the course of a long-evening-after a talk. Time and again I have heard him say that he just wrote it off, that it just came to him, and that he set it down as it came.

Once at Bread Loaf, however, I heard him add one very essential piece to the discussion of how it "just came." One night, he said, he had sat down after supper to work at a long piece of blank verse. The piece never worked out, but Mr. Frost found himself so absorbed in it that, when next he looked up, dawn was at his window. He rose, crossed to the window, stood looking out for a few minutes, and *then* it was that "Stopping by Woods" suddenly "just came," so that all he had to do was cross the room and write it down.

Robert Frost is the sort of artist who hides his traces. I know of no Frost worksheets anywhere. If someone has raided his wastebasket in secret, it is possible that such worksheets exist somewhere, but Frost would not willingly allow anything but the finished product to leave him. Almost certainly, therefore, no one will ever know what was in that piece of unsuccessful blank verse he had been working at with such concentration, but I for one would stake my life that could that worksheet be uncovered, it would be found to contain the germinal stuff of "Stopping by Woods"; that what was a-simmer in him all night without finding its proper form, suddenly, when he let his still-occupied mind look away, came at him from a different direction, offered itself in a different form, and that finding that form exactly right the impulse proceeded to marry itself to the new shape in one of the most miraculous performances of English lyricism.

And that, too—whether or not one can accept so hypothetical a discussion—is part of HOW the poem means. It means that marriage to the perfect form, the poem's shapen declaration of itself, its moment's monument fixed beyond all possibility of change. And thus, finally, in every truly good poem, "How does it mean?" must always be answered "Triumphantly." Whatever the poem "is about," *how* it means is always how Genesis means: the word become a form, and the form become a thing, and—when the becoming is true—the thing become a part of the knowledge and experience of the race forever.

The Meaning of "Acceptance"

Rita M. Defusio

Rita M. Defusio, a Robert Frost scholar, wrote this
piece as her master's thesis at Prince of Wales College in Canada. In addition to providing a line-by-
line reading of "Acceptance," one of Frost's well-
known poems, she explains how Frost bridged the
romantic poets of the 1800s to the late modernist
poets of this century.

After reading Frost's "Acceptance," I was almost as intrigued
with the title as with the poem itself. Since it was a sonnet, I
expected it to treat some solemn stereotyped topic, such as
"accepting the cross you have to carry" or "accepting a serious illness." Instead, here was a poem which used a *bird* as
its central figure. Why, then, wasn't its title "The Thrush,"
"The Nightingale" or the like? I was confused. Turning to my
dictionary for inspiration, I found that according to Webster's, acceptance means "the act of taking (what is offered
or given) willingly; agreeing to take the responsibilities of a
job, etc." It then occurred to me that, through this sonnet, a
number of parties may or may not be "accepting": the bird is
not the only one. By choosing a natural setting for his poem,
using the central figure of a bird, and grappling with questions that poets have long struggled with, Frost is accepting
his responsibilities as a poet—but only on his own terms,
and not without reservations. It is true that Frost draws on a
rich heritage of poetic thought; nevertheless, by modifying
conventional imagery, he asks us to be cautious of these
myths. It is up to us, then, to judge and accept his words.

BRIDGING THE ROMANTICS AND MODERNISTS

At the onset, we seem to be on familiar ground: the poem is
set at dusk, a time which (judging by the works of Keats and

Excerpted from Rita M. Defusio, Master's Thesis, November 1990. Reprinted with permission of the author.

Wordsworth, among others) traditionally seems to be most conducive to poetic images. Moreover, the speaker's initial description of the sunset contains strong echoes of "The Darkling Thrush." Frost's speaker describes sunset as a time "when the spent sun throws up its rays on cloud/And goes down burning into the gulf below" (1,2); we are reminded of Hardy's dauntless, aged thrush that "fling[s] his soul upon the growing gloom." Still, we immediately sense breaks from convention, as well: note how Frost's choice of the singular "cloud" versus the more conventional plural changes the sense of the sunset from mundane to almost mystical. However, the speaker mixes in more earthy terms, too: a "spent" sun sounds especially hopeless since the monetary connotations of "getting and spending" intensify the disturbing effect—business is alien to nature. Moreover, there is something less optimistic in Frost's term "throws up" than in Hardy's "flings": flinging can be seen as an act of joy or defiance, whereas we connect "throws up" with "throwing up one's hands" in defeat or disgust, or even in the grosser sense as a involuntary reflex and disgorging in times of sickness (e.g. Eliot's "The memory throws up high and dry" in his "Rhapsody on a Windy Night"). This is the first of a series of what I will call "howevers" that we encounter while reading this poem: we are constantly compelled to analyze and re-analyze the poem, for Frost chooses words and images that are charged with double-meanings. For example, although the fiery colors of a sunset are glorious, there is something disquieting in the phrase "goes down burning." As modern readers, we may connect this image with that of a plane crash, or with the more classical tragic image of Icarus, who went down burning into the sea.

Frost's speaker goes on to tell us that unlike in the case of the Thrush, the Nightingale, or the Cuckoo, in this setting "no voice in nature is heard to cry aloud/at what has happened [sunset]" (3,4): no one—man nor beast nor bird—verbalizes his emotions. There is no "saying," "caroling," "requiem" or "tale of visionary hours": silence reigns. We perceive the absence of voices as strange; the speaker seems to share that view. Accordingly, he then makes a curious observation:

Birds, at least, must know
It is the change to darkness in the sky.
Murmuring something quiet in her breast,
One bird begins to close a faded eye (4–7).

Consider the line "birds, at least, must know": the framing of "at least" makes it possible to read it in two ways. The speaker may be saying that "even if the birds here are lowly and non-singing, they *have* to realize it's night-time"; or it may mean that if any creatures are in tune with nature, *birds* are [as in Hardy's "some blessed Hope, whereof he knew" ("Thrush," 31)]. In any event, Frost seems to be trying to break with the convention of depicting birds as mythical, ageless creatures. Although he does not dismiss the myths, he is certainly wary of them. Hardy, too, used this break from convention in his "Darkling Thrush," by describing a bird that is indeed "built for death." Although he sings in the midst of bleakness, he is aged; moreover, the very wording of the poem suggests that Hardy may be parodying the glorification of bird imagery used by his predecessors (e.g. the grandiosity of "At once a voice arose among" or frivolity of "his happy good night air"). Frost's speaker tells us that these birds are not supernatural: they have basic physical needs, such as sleep, to rejuvenate a "faded eye." Also, far from the Wordsworthian ideal of "bringing tales of visionary hours," Frost's bird merely "murmur[s] something quiet in her breast": it mumbles only to itself, and shares nothing of itself with man. As such, it is just a bird—not a clear voice, and certainly not "blessed." Although we do not know what that "'something quiet" is, the bird is (for now) based mostly in the physical world . . . or is it? We recall that Frost himself has wondered about what constitutes "somethingness" before: it may be an infinitesimal object—or it may be Truth! Further, there is something dream-like and magical about the word "murmur": its hushed quality conjures up images of the street lamp which hums "La lune ne garde aucune . . ." in Eliot's work. We are also reminded of the darkened world of another being, Keats' "Nightingale," who dwells among the hypnotic "murmurous haunt of flies on summer eves" (50). Yet unlike the nightingale, who experiences no evil in his sensual realm, a bird in Frost's setting faces some degree of danger or urgency: "overtaken too far from his nest,/ hurrying low above the grove, some waif/swoops just in time to his remembered tree" (8–10). The implication is that the setting must not be idyllic, for then the birds could stay out all night without care for time or harm. In previous poems that used birds as central figures, we never felt any fear for the birds' safety—here, we do and so does the "waif" itself:

[The bird] swoops just in time to his remembered tree.
At most he thinks or twitters softly, 'Safe!
Now let the night be dark for all of me.
Let the night be too dark for me to see
Into the future. Let what will be, be' (10–14).

These lines which close the sonnet are packed with potential meaning. Note how Frost, through his speaker, qualifies the bird in line 11. No sooner does he call the bird by a name most often used to refer to humans (waif), and allows the bird to "think," than he makes us doubt that birds are capable of thought—perhaps, he concedes, they can only "twitter." This line is reminiscent of Hardy's "The Last Chrysanthemum," where, after waxing poetic about the flower, he suddenly pulls back and declares "I talk as if the thing were born/with sense to work its mind" (21–22). In both cases, we are left to wonder if the flower/bird can think or not. However, what may be most thought-provoking are the words of the bird itself. As it nestles down for the night, the bird expresses relief that it is safe, then thinks (or twitters) "Now let the night be dark for *all of me*" (emphasis mine). Again, we are faced with two possible interpretations. The bird may be totally self-absorbed to the point that it cares nothing for its fellows as long as it is safe; on the other hand, it may be sophisticated, seeing itself as part of a collective whole, as one that is representative of "birdness." Because it feels this connection so strongly, the bird apparently has no fears about other members of his species; as far as the bird is concerned, if it is safe then "birdness" is safe, and it can rest. This strong identification with a "whole" is also alluded to in Yeats' "The Lake Isle of Innisfree," where he says that he will have "a hive for the honey bee." In both cases, we get a strong sense of camaraderie or connectedness when the poet uses a singular noun to describe something tribal.

Thus, the impending darkness does not concern the bird. He seems almost happy to be ignorant of what will come in the future, whether the future which he will not "see into" be as close as later that evening or more distant. In the darkening state of drowsiness that the bird is entering, conventional time seems be cast aside; as a result, the bird's cares are cast aside as well. We are reminded of Keats' "Ode to a Nightingale" where he tells us that, once in the nightingale's sensual world: "there is no light, . . . I cannot see what flowers are at my feet." (38,41). However, we know that Keats cannot remain in the realm of the nightingale, because he, like all men, is time-bound. Upon seeing that even the beautiful things in the nightingale's world, such as violets, are "fast-fading," we realize what Keats is implying: to be part of the natural world is to be mortal. In fact, at the end of his "Ode," Keats raises the same questions that Frost does when Frost wonders if the bird "thinks" or "twitters": after he hears the nightingale's song fade as it flies away, Keats asks "Was it a vision, or a waking dream?/Fled is that music:—do I wake or sleep?" (79,80). Keats wonders if there can ever be something transcendent in the natural world, or if he is merely imposing a false idea onto the nightingale. We wonder how Frost's bird can afford to be so confident. In the closing words, we may find some clues.

Consider, finally, the last sentiments of Frost's bird: "Let what will be, be." Perhaps taking a cue from Eliot once more, Frost ends his poem with a cliché. It is in this cliché, however, that we find the most loaded language in the entire poem. Perhaps the bird in "Acceptance" is ultimately attempting to clear up the "deception of the thrush"—a clarification that was begun by his counterpart in Eliot's "Burnt Norton":

Go . . . human kind
Cannot bear very much reality.
Time past and time future
What might have been and what had been
Point to one end, which is always present (44–48)

Eliot's bird tells us that we cannot bear reality—but what *is* reality? Ironically, it seems to be the created "reality" that was defined by Eliot's poetic predecessors: those reflected, in a glimpse, in the concrete pool. These poets attempted to marry (or at least reconcile) the ideal and the real, to define and make visible what is invisible and transcendent. They did so by describing their visions in familiar mythical and metaphorical language, using images such as birds and Eden-like settings. Eliot's bird seems to be saying that dwelling in the past—in this poem's sense, by merely recycling old poetic ideas—is not sufficient. Although thoughts of what "might have been" and paradigms will surely be with us, we cannot dwell solely in their world any more than we can dwell in the kingdom of the mythical nightingale. Eliot's bird implies that the past as defined by our poetic ancestors is valuable to us insofar as it gives us a basis for creating *newer* definitions of life. Men, poets and otherwise, should best be concerned with "now;" after all, though the past has affected us and the future will affect us, we must live in the present. Therefore, when Frost's bird says "Let what will be, be" before it falls asleep, we can read it not only in its conventional sense, as an acceptance of the future, but also as an implicit faith in the poetry of now—questions and all.

Does the bird sleep so easily because it is carefree? No. We have seen that it faces dangers in the natural world. Its attitude must come from something else. Is it at peace because it has deceived itself after all, and has chosen sleep as a means of ignoring an inevitable future? Is it at peace because it is a dumb animal? Or, is it at peace because it knows something (a Truth?) that we humans don't—how to accept reality as it is, and still be content? Frost allows—perhaps, *encourages*—the questions to remain. It seems that in formulating the text of the poem, and in utilizing the images to do so, the ideas and language of Frost's poetic predecessors rise up as surely as the figures that were behind the speaker in "Burnt Norton"—they have become a part of his psyche as a poet, and ours as readers of poetry. In Jungian terms, they have become a part of our collective unconscious, as inescapable as our own thoughts. What Frost has done in "Acceptance" is to have indeed accepted the clay of images and questions left to him by the poets who came before him; then, however, he has gone a step further, and moulded these images into newer shapes and ideas for us to ponder.

The Biographical Nature of "The Lovely Shall Be Choosers"

Theodore Morrison

Theodore Morrison, a writer and close friend of Frost's, analyzes the poem Frost wrote about his mother, "The Lovely Shall Be Choosers," examining its biographical nature. Morrison suggests that Frost's mother's praise of him as a boy—"that Rob can do anything"—gave him the confidence to be a poet.

The only way to describe a man so complex as Robert Frost is to say that he was a bundle of paradoxes, that he was made up of pairs of opposites, both of which were true of him at the same time. He was, for example, a great man who contained a small man. His intellectual endowment, even apart from poetry, was immense, and at his best he had a wide and sympathetic humanity. He was also capable of seeing enemies where none existed, capable of nursing grudges and sulking over fancied slights. He gave an impression of magnificent sanity, as firmly grounded as a granite slab, and this impression was not false; yet in private his complicated balance, as complicated as the motions of a gyroscopic top, could be so disturbed as barely to recover its perilous equilibrium.

Another paradox appears in the first stanza of "Revelation," a little poem in his first book:

> We make ourselves a place apart
>   Behind light words that tease and flout,
> But oh, the agitated heart
>   Till someone really find us out.

Frost wanted to be found out—by the right people in the right way. The agitation of his heart to be discovered was intense and did not cease to the end of his life. The man who in his later years became not only an American but an international public figure, who became a father image to television

Excerpted from Theodore Morrison, "The Agitated Heart," *The Atlantic Monthly*, July 1977. Reprinted by permission of Anne Morrison Smyth.

viewers who had never opened one of his books, used light and not-so-light words to tease and flout, both privately and on the platform, and made himself a place apart behind their shelter. But in the very act of hiding he wanted to reveal himself to those who could see him as he wanted to be seen. He craved a kind of ideal sharing of his poems, a total, intuitive transfer of the poem to the mind of a sympathetic reader or listener, without meddling intervention by study, explication, or dogged analysis. He also craved a similar sharing of his life. Frost was obsessed by his own life. As his biographer, Lawrance Thompson, has pointed out, and as those who knew him were sharply aware, he told many of its episodes over and over again. He was his own Horatio, and in this harsh world drew his breath—in pain, yes; also in pleasure, in wonder, and in a constant battle of self-justification—to tell his story. When the mood was on him, he could spill out confidences with a recklessness the very opposite of the man who made himself a place apart and hid his tracks by teasing and flouting.

In a tart admonition to Sidney Cox, quoted in Lawrance Thompson's *Selected Letters,* Frost informs his friend, "I have written to keep the over curious out of the secret places of my mind both in my verse and in my letters to such as you." Warning enough to any interpreter! Yet it remains true also that he wanted to make his revelation, both in and out of poetry, and to be found out, in his own way, on his own terms. He himself has not only revealed but exposed himself to an astonishing extent, in talk and in letters, for better and for worse. Nothing can prevent the continuing scrutiny of the evidence as it comes to hand, and if much of the scrutiny would be distasteful to him if he could return to us, yet as long as he continued to be Robert Frost he would veer between covering his tracks and laying them so that the right people could follow his trail.

In his later life Frost was accused of casting himself in a role, making himself a legend, acting a part, adopting a persona. The charge was usually brought against him as a public performer, but has . . . been extended to the voice we hear in his poems, as though that were an equally nurtured artifice. On the face of it, in view of the television appearances, the films, the press interviews, the showmanship of his readings, the charge against his public manner can claim a good deal of support. The evidence makes it plausible. Yet to many of those who knew him well, the case is subtler and more difficult than any such one-sided statement of it. And when the charge is carried over to the poems, it becomes even more questionable. If it were true in any deep-rooted or distinctive way, the poems would cease to ring true, and they don't.

What we confront, in trying to deal with charges of this sort, is another of the paradoxes in the man, the pairs of opposites, each true at once. Frost says in one of his letters that no one who is affected can write really well. He had his affectations—who hasn't? Mrs. Morrison and I used to smile when during World War II Frost would tax Churchill with affecting a Cockney accent, as though Frost himself never affected the rustic. He began one of his most brilliant and delicately felt discourses at the Bread Loaf Writers' Conference with the words, "It says in the Bible, or if it don't, it oughta. . . ." No doubt my memory exaggerates, but he certainly did *not* say, "It says in the Bible, or if it doesn't, it ought to. . . ." No doubt he artfully split the difference in the way that made his spoken remarks so inordinately hard to transcribe in print. Yet despite his calculated manner on occasion, he was in a large sense one of the most unaffected men anyone could hope to encounter. He began another Bread Loaf discourse, shortly after the death of Mrs. Frost, by saying that he had lately kept in his pocket some object he could finger while he talked on the platform, to remind himself that he was the same man in public as in private. Recently, he added, the object had been a thorn. In a curious way, despite the showmanship he learned gradually over the years, he *was* the same man in public as in private. He had the same crotchets, spites, defensiveness through humor and pun and witticism and plain wisecrack, the same greatness and fertility of imagination. His conversation, at dinner table and in private, was "all of a piece throughout" with the man who spoke on the platform, the man who wrote the poems, except, of course, that the poems arrived at formal perfection—they had *that* kind of artifice—while the talk was half conveyed by a spectrum of gesture and by the expressive play of loose flesh over the magnificent structure of his skull.

Naturally, Frost's poems are full of the dramatic. He is dramatic in that he can create characters who are not mere phases of his own sensibility. He is dramatic in the stricter sense that a surprising number of his narratives make natural stage pieces as they stand. No one ever emphasized more than he did the element of play in literature. I used to think he emphasized it to excess, often as a covert form of his peculiar defensiveness, a way of keeping "the over curious out of the secret places" of his mind. If we undertake to see the man in his work, we must make ample allowance (as I cannot do here) for the places where biography is *not* significantly present, as well as trying to understand it where it is.

FROST THE MAN

Perhaps enough has been said on the complexities and paradoxes of Frost the man to serve as prelude to an examination of a particular group of his poems. These are poems in which he may at first seem out of character, very different from the accepted impression of him, or in which his life is a powerful though concealed presence, or in which he approaches the esoteric—a word which may surprise Frost readers, but which has its application.

Of course, Frost is not esoteric in the sense of having a private doctrine to peddle through a circle of initiates, but I think it fair to say that he comes close to the esoteric when he publishes a poem that cannot be understandingly read without clues divulged to friends. Such a poem is "The Lovely Shall Be Choosers." The general scheme of the action in this poem stands out clearly enough, but its treatment in detail is sufficiently secretive and allusive so that it has misled both private readers and public commentators.

A woman of dignity and beauty is to be punished for her choice in marriage, the consequences of which do not lie within her foresight or control. The punishment is to be carried out by joys which form an ironic parallel to the seven joys of Mary, ironic because each joy is a grim compensation for pain and humiliation. The progressive punishment takes place in an eerie metaphysical frame. The poem, except for a single passage of description, consists of a dialogue between "The Voice," who is supreme in the poem, and "Voices," who are obviously subordinate agents of the omnipotent Voice, his officers appointed to carry out the relentless chastisement. The place that punishment occupied in Frost's mind deserves a word. Punished physically and severely himself in childhood by his father, Frost could not exclude from his view of things a sort of metaphysical sense of the rightness or ultimacy of the punitive. The God, or "Voice," who rules in the world of "The Lovely Shall Be

Choosers" speaks with a note of outright authoritarian sarcasm in the lines: "She *would* refuse love safe with wealth and honor! / The lovely shall be choosers, shall they?" Yet, and this is of highest importance to the poem, the Voice that orders the lovely chooser hurled seven levels down the world by means of seven joys that are so many pains also orders that at every stage she shall be left blameless.

ART IMITATES LIFE

The woman was Frost's mother, to whom he was peculiarly close. Frost made the identification himself, more than once, to more than one person. Mrs. Morrison has said to me and others that in all the uncounted hours she spent as Frost's secretary, listening to him disburden himself of his life, past and present, while often enough she ached to get an important letter written or an essential decision made, his mother was the one human being of whom she never heard Frost say an ill word. We could hardly guess how many times, after one of his public triumphs in later life, we have heard him repeat, with doggerel emphasis that did not conceal how much he meant by it, the words of the old song or catch he could not forget: "I wish my mother could see me now." Those who think his platform manner was entirely a calculated artifice could well give a thought to this telltale refrain. He slept in his mother's room until at least well into his high school years. Another of the paradoxes in this man of complexity was the combination in him of something very like mother fixation with the full measure of virility he brought to his marriage.

His own marriage is a subsequent story. About the marriage of his parents, Frost formed a suspicion that in retrospect can be viewed only with a certain amusement. For a long time Frost misdated his birth, making himself younger by a year than he actually was. After the death of his father, Frost's mother brought him and his younger sister from San Francisco to live with the Frost grandparents in Lawrence, Massachusetts. Frost believed, justly or not—for the poem the *belief* is what matters—that his grandparents looked down on his mother, and even by insinuation accused her of luring or perhaps trapping his father into marriage. He suspected that as the first child he might have arrived unconventionally early. This suspicion pretty plainly underlies the first of the ironic joys in the poem: "Be her first joy her wedding, / That though a wedding, / Is yet—well something they know, he and she."

The second joy introduces the friends among whom she stood, proud herself and a pride to them, in the one descriptive passage in the poem, friends left behind at a distance when Mrs. Frost followed her husband to San Francisco. Among them, one supposes, was the man she might have married "safe with wealth and honor." Her second joy is plainly called a "grief"; its only joy is that she can keep it secret. The friends know nothing of it to make it "shameful." And her third joy is that although now they cannot help knowing, "They move in pleasure too far off / To think much or much care."

What was this grief that might have put her in a shameful light to the far-off friends? The same suspicion that led Frost to misdate his birth may continue to be at work in the second and third joys, but it seems plain that another motif enters as well. Frost learned of, or at least came to believe in, his father's infidelity, or at any rate indiscreet conduct. His sense of his mother's humiliation by his father's public attentions to another woman may well be the chief element in the two joys that turn on her grim comfort in knowing that her friends were too remote and preoccupied to think much of her. She had indeed chosen, as it turned out, the opposite of love safe with wealth and honor.

SUCCEEDING JOYS

The succeeding joys, through the sixth, deal progressively with the unhappy satisfaction of pride. Give her a child at either knee so that she may tell them once, unforgettably, how she used to walk in brightness, but give her new friends so that she dare not tell, knowing her story would not be believed. Then give her the painful joy of pride that she never stooped to tell. Then make her among the humblest seem even less than they are.

Why should Isabel Moodie Frost have come to seem, at least as her son imagined her case, less than the humblest? Isabel Moodie seems to have been a beautiful and gifted woman, but her gifts were intellectual and spiritual. They did not extend to dressing smartly or keeping house in a meticulous New England fashion or disciplining rowdy children in a schoolroom. Her sixth joy is the comfort of knowing that her way of life, as a widow trying in pinched circumstances to bring up two children by schoolteaching, is one she comes to from too high too late to learn.

Her seventh and final joy turns on the word *one*, italicized by Frost himself in the printed text. "Then send some *one* with eyes to see . . . And words to wonder in her hearing how she came there / But without time to linger for her story." I have no express warrant in anything I ever heard Frost say for asserting that this *one* is Robert himself, Isabel Moodie's son, but this interpretation is so natural as to be inevitable. What is the whole poem except the poet's vision of his mother's life? We must keep in mind that while in substance the poem is retrospective, a vision of a woman's life after the fact, in form it is anticipatory. The Voice is giving orders to the Voices that they are to carry out over a period of twenty years. "How much time have we?" / "Take twenty years. . . ." Of course this figure is a round number, but by two decades, give or take a little, after Isabel Moodie's marriage—the central *choice* from which everything follows—her son could well have been old enough to make surmises about his mother's life, old enough to "wonder in her hearing how she came there." And by the same token his own expanding life, the battles of late adolescence or early manhood, would deprive him of "time to linger for her story." Time and growth were needed if he was to be "sent" on this particular mission of understanding, yet time and growth defeat the mission, so that her seventh joy is "her heart's going out to this one / So that she almost speaks." Almost. She is left with the barren pride of never in fact telling "how once she walked in brightness," never directly telling even the son to whom her heart went out, as Isabel Moodie's unquestionably did to her son, Robert Frost. "That Rob can do anything" was a refrain she spoke often in his hearing, and that he himself often repeated to others.

IMAGINARY CHARACTERS

What happens to the poem when the reader is given the necessary clues? Surely the gain in clearness does not destroy but deepens and vindicates the mysterious and visionary power of "The Lovely Shall Be Choosers." The poem is as truly a feat of imagination as if it had been written about an altogether fictitious character and not about the poet's mother. All characters become imaginary in the act of being imagined, and in this sense Isabel Moodie becomes an imaginary character in the poem devoted to her. The poem, which is not without a strain of bitterness and of guilt, *is* a metaphysical vision. But we do not have real access to the content of the vision until we know who the characters are, and when we know, it is not merely a persona or mask we hear speaking. It is the actual son of an actual mother, since the son happens to be a poet.

The Use of Light in Robert Frost's "The Death of the Hired Man"

Elizabeth Fitzsimons

In this selection, Elizabeth Fitzsimons analyzes the motif of light in "The Death of the Hired Man." Fitzsimons chooses to focus on Mary as the pivotal character in the poem and emphasizes the parallels between the earthly Mary in the poem and the divine Mary of Christianity. Fitzsimons is a student at Boston College.

The use of light throughout Robert Frost's poem "The Death of the Hired Man" is strikingly symbolic. The natural light of the moon and use of artificial light surrounds Mary and differentiates her from the darkness. The name Mary, given to the only female in the poem, in and of itself alludes to the historical and religious woman who gave birth to Jesus, "The Light" of the world, and who is Mother of God.

At three different points during the poem we see Mary spotlighted by light against a backdrop of utter darkness. Light is used to put a bright focus on Mary and project many of her qualities in the goodness of pure light. In the first line Mary is "musing on the lamp-lame at the table." She is not concerning herself with the terror of the surrounding darkness on the rural plane. Instead, she gazes at the undulating flame of light and contemplates the radiating light.

The second use of light occurs just before Mary and Warren try to define "home." Each of them however, come to different conclusions about the meaning of home. Frost writes, as if to foreshadow the event,

Part of a moon was falling down the west,
Dragging the whole sky with it to the hills.
Its light poured softly in her lap. She saw it
And spread her apron to it.

Reprinted from Elizabeth Fitzsimons, "The Use of Light in Robert Frost's 'The Death of the Hired Man,'" unpublished paper, April 30, 1998, by permission of the author.

The light in this case is not just energy, but it has transformed into a physical thing. It streams down from the sky to illuminate Mary standing in the kitchen. While the moon seems to disappear so does the reality of their environment. The light is strong and comes from a disappearing source casting darkness onto the sky and hills. While spotlighting Mary the light touches her "softly" and caresses her apron. She is a receptacle for the light and actually preserves it in the starkness of night when light is absent. In this light Mary's merciful and compassionate ways are highlighted.

The third glow of light shines when Warren ventures into the house to check on Silas, the hired man. Mary waits for her husband to return while watching to see "if that small sailing cloud / Will hit or miss the moon." The reader is then told:

> It hit the moon.
> Then there were three there, making a dim row,
> The moon, the little silver cloud, and she.

The "dim row" is apparent to foreshadow the darkness which will present itself in Silas's death. The moon, cloud, and Mary are no longer vivid because they are now "dim." The description of light disassociates Mary from the utter darkness of the upcoming earthly death. It places Mary at a point of projection whereby light filters from her and provides a line from the heavens to earth.

Mary as Religious Symbol

Mary is beyond earthly obligations. This statement has a double meaning because it is true for Mary the woman in the poem and Mary the mother of Jesus. Mary, the only female in the poem, contrasts with all four male characters in the poem who are earth-bound. Silas's banker brother is consumed with concepts of family, influence, and wealth. Wilson is tied to notions of intellect and expanding his mind while Silas only understands haying. Finally, Warren is a religious man who emerges from darkness in the beginning and enters back into it in the end with the [discovery] of Silas's death. Mary is the only character who is associated with light. We see this in the three instances of the flickering lamp, falling moon, and silver cloud. It is evident that the ever changing forces of the sky illuminate the poem. Mary embodies the ultimate vision of light. She is utterly open and will not be bound by social class. She is willing to help Silas.

Mary is aware of her personal duties and acts with compassion and embracing love when dealing with Silas.

Frost ends the poem with the word "Dead" as said by Warren, who is already surrounded by darkness. However, before the reader encounters this final overbearing darkness of death, the reader has experienced, even just for a few moments, the luminescence of the sky with the help of Mary. While death is ultimately inevitable Mary proves to the reader that we do not need to live our lives concerning ourselves with the narrow confusions of the "hired man" or with the self-motivated actions of the banker and professor. We must realize the inescapability of our journey through the dark and strive like Mary to become part of the light. We must make our existence on earth a place where Mary is our paradigm and we desire to allow love and light to flourish.

"Design" and Frost's Sonnets

Elaine Barry

Elaine Barry, a well-known literary critic, examines Frost and the sonnet form in this excerpt. Sonnets were most popular in Shakespeare's time, but Frost revolutionized the form: He spent a year practicing how to write them. Barry notes how the tightness and poetic demands of the fourteen-line poem bring order to the chaos of many of Frost's "dark" themes. She analyzes Frost's sonnet "Design," considered one of the best sonnets ever written.

In a letter that Frost wrote to the American critic Lewis Chase in 1917, he listed some of his favorite poets and concluded the list with the comment: "But before all write me as one who cares most for the Shakespearean and Wordsworthian sonnets." His own poetry reflects this preference. Frost probably wrote more first-rate sonnets than any other poet of this century; "Mowing," "Design," "Once by the Pacific," "The Oven Bird," "Range-Finding," "Putting in the Seed," "Acquainted with the Night," "Meeting and Passing," and "The Silken Tent," are among them. More succinctly than his other lyrics, Frost's sonnets illustrate his abiding concern for questions of form and metaphor.

His partiality for such a disciplined form at a time when poetry was moving away from conscious structure is a complex matter. It is related not only to his classical taste but, in a deeper way, to his psychological need for inner discipline as a way of coping with the chaotic forces of life itself. The insanity of his sister, the emotional instability of his daughter Irma, the depressions that led to his son's suicide and that made Frost himself "scared" of his own "desert places"—these were all tragic personal evidence of what could follow from the loss of an inner structure.

Thus, when Frost speaks of "form," the word has two levels of reference. On one level, it refers to all those elements of traditional prosody—rhyme, rhythm, meter, stanza pattern—with which he never ceased to be preoccupied. Indeed, the common sense of his technical statements about poetry—his ideas, for example, on the "sound of sense," on rhyming, on dramatic context, on the straining of rhythm and meter—tell us more about the real nature of the artistic process than more pretentious concepts such as Eliot's "objective correlative" or F.R. Leavis's "felt experience." Such prosodic concerns were, for Frost, the essence of writing poetry. Free verse, he claimed, was like "playing tennis with the net down." And each of these technical concerns was called into highly conscious play by the sonnet form.

FORM BRINGS ORDER TO CHAOS

But on a deeper, more philosophical level, Frost saw "form" as the cohering mental process behind all these technical elements. It is the catalyst by which chaos ("the vast chaos of all I have lived through") becomes meaning. As he wrote to the Amherst student newspaper in 1935:

> We people are thrust forward out of the suggestions of form in the rolling clouds of nature. In us nature reaches its height of form and through us exceeds itself. When in doubt there is always form for us to go on with. Anyone who has achieved the least form to be sure of it, is lost to the larger excruciations. I think it must stroke faith the right way....
>
> The background is hugeness and confusion shading away from where we stand into black and utter chaos; and against the background any small man-made figure of order and concentration.

Frost thus gives "form" the widest possible definition. It is the principle of order in the whole physical universe, by means of which the potential dissipation of the "rolling clouds of nature" is averted and channeled into the creation of man, a being with an intelligence capable, in turn, of controlling nature. In the "chaotic" welter of impressions and emotions in any individual life, it is only "form" that can shape such chaos into a direction and a meaning. In a poem, it is "form" alone that transmutes the vague intuition (the "lump in the throat") in which any poem has its origin into something that is understandable and communicable (a "clarification of life"). What all these aspects of form have in common is a tough-minded discipline. Not surprisingly, Frost was fond of making a parallel between athletic prowess and the writing of poetry: both are "performances," gaining their victories through stern rigor.

METAPHOR

Close to this concept of form is Frost's concept of metaphor, to which he also gave the widest possible definition. Every creative thought rests on metaphor, he claimed, because every important thought is a "feat of association," "saying one thing in terms of another."

Metaphor is the intellectual principle by which the "tantalizing vagueness" of any creative intuition—be it scientific or artistic—finds its thought and takes communicable shape. To illustrate the point, Frost himself used metaphors to define what he meant by the term. Metaphor, he claimed, is a "prism" that takes raw "enthusiasm" and spreads it on a "screen," so that what had been simply a matter of feeling thus becomes a matter of perception. Or, in a more homely analogy, it is a napkin ring: "Like a napkin, we fold the thought, squeeze it through the ring, and it expands once more." What is common to both these metaphoric definitions is a sense of strain or tension. All meaningful thought is hard won, demanding both discipline and detachment. "The only materialist," wrote Frost, ". . . is the man who gets lost in his material without a gathering metaphor to throw it into shape and order. He is the lost soul."

Form, then, creates meaning. And, in a very real sense, it is the meaning. Nothing demonstrates this more clearly than the concentrated form of the sonnet. Like Coleridge and Emerson, Frost believed that a poem was essentially organic. It creates itself, having been given direction from "the first line laid down"; or, as Frost expressed it in a memorable image: "Like a piece of ice on a hot stove, the poem must ride on its own melting." If a poem is simply written to a formula, or if it is written to build up to a previously chosen final line—if the "clarification," in other words, occurs before the poem has begun—then the rationale, the creative impetus, of the poem is gone, and the poem will be bad, dishonest.

> [The poet's] intention is of course a particular mood that won't be satisfied with anything less than its own fulfillment. . . . One thing to know it by: it shrinks shyly from anticipatory expression. Tell love beforehand and, as Blake says,

it loses flow without filling the mould; the cast will be a re-ject. The freshness of a poem belongs absolutely to its not having been thought out and then set to verse. . . . A poem is the emotion of having a thought while the reader waits a lit-tle anxiously for the success of dawn. The only discipline to begin with is the inner mood that at worst may give the poet a false start or two like the almost microscopic filament of cotton that goes before the blunt thread-end and must be picked up first by the eye of the needle.

LIMITS

To a certain extent, any poet who is struggling to fulfill such an inner mood will have his expression determined, perhaps even limited, by the techniques that belong to his craft. Like the painter or the musician, the poet has only a certain num-ber of tools available to him. If he is writing in English, Frost would say, he has basically a choice of two meters (Frost re-fused to acknowledge more than "strict iambic" and "loose iambic"); he has a choice of "any length of line up to six feet"; and he can use "an assortment of line lengths for any shape of stanza." Not much with which to do battle with chaos or to fulfill an inner mood that is crying for articula-tion. But more than adequate if the poet has enough faith to put himself in league with his own tools. Frost illustrated this creative determinism of form beautifully with reference to one of Shakespeare's sonnets:

Suppose him to have written down "When in disgrace with Fortune and men's eyes." He has uttered about as much as he has to live up to in the theme as in the form. Odd how the two advance into the open pari passu. He has given out that he will descend into Hades, but he has confided in no one how far be-fore he will turn back, or whether he will turn back at all, and by what jutting points of rock he will pick his way. He may proceed as in blank verse. Two lines more, however, and he has let himself in for rhyme, three more and he has set him-self a stanza. Up to this point his discipline has been the self-discipline whereof it is written in so great praise. The harsher discipline from without is now well begun. He who knows not both knows neither. His wordly commitments are now three or four deep. Between us, he was no doubt bent on the sonnet in the first place from habit, and what's the use in pretending he was a freer agent than he had any ambition to be? He had made most of his commitments all in one plunge. The only suspense he asks us to share with him is in the theme. He goes down, for instance, to a depth that must surprise him as much as it does us. But he doesn't even have the say of how long his piece will be. Any worry is as to whether he will outlast or last out the fourteen lines—have to cramp or stretch to come out even—have enough bread for the butter or butter for the bread. As a matter of fact, he gets through in twelve lines and doesn't know quite what to do with the last two. . . .

"DESIGN"

A later sonnet, "Design," has far more intellectual tautness.

I found a dimpled spider, fat and white,
On a white heal-all, holding up a moth
Like a white piece of rigid satin cloth—
Assorted characters of death and blight
Mixed ready to begin the morning right,
Like the ingredients of a witches' broth—
A snow-drop spider, a flower like a froth,
And dead wings carried like a paper kite.

What had that flower to do with being white,
The wayside blue and innocent heal-all?
What brought the kindred spider to that height,
Then steered the white moth thither in the night?
What but design of darkness to appall?—
If design govern in a thing so small.

Here the metaphor is carried much further than a simple parallel and an expression of wonder at it. The central image of the "design," in its conjunction of the spider, the flower (a white heal-all) and the moth, . . . becomes the focus for a subtle questioning of one of the traditional arguments for the existence of God—the argument that, just as a clock implies a clockmaker, so the evident design in the physical world implies a Designer. This reasoning is commonly known as the "argument from design."

The basic structure of "Design" is Petrarchan; the situation is presented in the octet and resolved, after a definite break, in the sestet. But the structure also follows the traditional sequence of logical debate: first the presentation of the facts, then the questioning of them, then the resolution. The scheme, revolving around only four rhymes, is even tighter and more concentrated than in most Petrarchan sonnets. It is as if the terrifying implications of meaninglessness that the poem hints at demanded a highly disciplined form to bring them within the domain of human comprehension. The greater the threat of dissipation in the subject, the tighter the conscious form needed to hold it in. "Design" has an aptness of form that is absolutely faultless.

The octet presents, without any authorial comment, a simple nature scene: a spider and a moth on a white flower in the morning freshness. Deliberately, it builds up the impression of normality; the whole impact of the sestet would be lost if we simply accepted this scene as an aberration. If the poem is to be a wicked reversal of the argument from design, then it must challenge that argument by its own logic. It therefore concedes the immediate point. An apparent design in all things implies an original Designer. Granted. But if the apparent design is one of horror, what kind of Designer? What immortal hand or eye dare frame the awful symmetry of this scene? The necessary impression of normality is created partly by the beautiful regularity of the form, partly by the cheery colloquialness of the speaker's tone ("mixed ready to begin the morning right"), but mostly by the careful choice of words that are usually associated with innocence and freshness ("dimpled," "white," "snowdrop," "froth," "satin").

Yet, undercutting this careful normality the effect is one of horror, just as the most chilling manifestation of insanity is the one that is camouflaged by an apparent rationality. Each element that helps to create the surface normality here is paradoxically, chillingly, negated by the context of the total "mixture." The regularity of form, for example, is mocked by the visual symmetry of this study in white. The colloquial tone creates a reassurance that is denied by the "appalling" scene that gradually unfolds. Finally, the innocuous words, when linked to this context, become horrifyingly perverted.

The first line rollicks along in perfectly regular iambics. "Dimpled" modifies any shock in finding the word "spider," and "fat" modifies it further. This is the kind of spider that Miss Muffet might have encountered. "White," given emphasis by ending the line, pulls us up. A white spider? Even if [Edgar Allan] Poe and [Herman] Melville had not previously attuned us to the ambiguities of whiteness, the disquieting contradiction here sounds the first jarring note. It rings again in the second line. The "heal-all" (so-called because of certain healing properties assigned to it) is a little blue flower found all over New England ("The wayside blue and innocent heal-all"). Here its very name contributes to the mockery of the poem, and its unusual albino form seems ominously unnatural, like that of the spider. The final ingredient in the scene is a moth, also "white," but white and "rigid" with the "satin" patina of death, and completely denaturalized, simply "like a . . . piece of . . . cloth."

The resonance of the words throughout the octet is extra-ordinary; the poem begins to reverberate on many levels of association. Note, for example, how the ritual action of the spider's "holding up" the moth makes him seem like the celebrant of a mass—not a black mass, despite the diabolism of the scene, but a perversely white one. The resonance continues in the three-line parenthesis (lines 4–6). "Assorted characters" suggests a group of strolling players acting out a ritual dance of death. They are "assorted," implying their separate identities, yet "mixed," implying a conscious (and diabolical) Mixer, the first thrust at the argument from design. "Mixed ready to begin the morning right." Even the obvious pun on "rite" cannot destroy the terrible heartiness here—like the terrible heartiness of Macbeth's witches presaging "so foul and fair a day." The summary of the scene in the last two lines of the octet refocuses and intensifies each ingredient. The spider is now "a snow-drop spider," its identity blurring into that of a flower. "A flower like a froth" sounds delicate and fluffy, except that "froth," partly because of the rhyme, has associations with the ominous "broth" of the witches. And the solemn spondees of "dead wings carried" sound a dirge for the victim of the little drama, now as transparent and skeletal as a "paper kite."

THE ARGUMENT

The facts having thus been marshaled, the "argument" proceeds with strict philosophical method in the sestet. The first question ("What had that flower to do with being white?") goes beyond ontology to question the whole notion of guilt or responsibility in a seemingly arbitrary world. The second ("What brought the kindred spider to that height, / Then steered the white moth thither in the night?") is more malicious; the word "steered" hints at a conscious Malevolence behind it all. The questions are resolved by a rhetorical question: "What but design of darkness to appall?" All the images of horrifying whiteness become fused in a "design of darkness." The concept of a Manichean universe, of a world created by the forces of darkness, is the only logical conclusion of this perverse argument from design.

But the poem does not end with the thirteenth line. The final line is a poetic tour de force, the whole poem moving relentlessly to its conclusion: "If design govern in a thing so small." "If" is the crucial word; it opens up two possible interpretations. Perhaps, it might be arguing, it is indeed fool-ish to use such a trivial scene as an argument for or against design; design does *not* govern in a thing so small. But if not there, where? The other possibility is terrifying—that there is no design at all in the world, not even a Manichean one. The whiteness simply mirrors an absurd blankness. The poem thus concludes with a philosophical checkmate.

"Design" is a poem of terror whichever way we look at it. And it achieves its impact by the very tautness of its expres-sion. What the sonnet form did was to set the rigorous boundaries to that expression. The challenge then was to tighten the ideas so that, within those boundaries, every word carries weight. Just how much Frost tightened his ideas may be seen clearly by comparing our present version of "Design" with its original version entitled "In White."

> A dented spider like a snowdrop white
> On a white Heal-all, holding up a moth
> Like a white piece of lifeless satin cloth—
> Saw ever curious eye so strange a sight?
> Portent in little, assorted death and blight
> Like the ingredients of a witches' broth?
> The beady spider, the flower like a froth,
> And the moth carried like a paper kite.
>
> What had that flower to do with being white,
> The blue Brunella every child's delight?
> What brought the kindred spider to that height?
> (Make we no thesis of the miller's plight.)
> What but design of darkness and of night?
> Design, design! Do I use the word aright?

How lame it all sounds! The central idea is there, though not the subtlety of the final twist. A few of the images are al-ready in place—"snowdrop," "satin cloth," the "witches' broth," "froth," and "paper kite." But the most obvious simi-larity is the form—not simply the choice of the sonnet, but the octet-sestet structure and the sequential argument. If Frost had dropped the notion of a sonnet and had continued to refine his argument into another stanza, "In White" would probably never have progressed beyond the barely compe-tent poem it is. Instead, given the limited number of lines and metrical feet in his chosen form, he concentrated on making each one of them count. Note, for example, how the substitution of "rigid" for "lifeless" in line 3 adds the sugges-tion of rigor mortis, or "dimpled" for "dented" in line 1 adds a babylike innocence that will later be dramatically undercut. "Brunella," as a name for the heal-all, and "miller" (a miller is a moth with powdery wings) are altogether too localized and coy. The change in line 13 from the pointlessly repetitive "design of darkness and of night" to "design of darkness to appall" is masterly; and Frost was too word conscious to have been unaware of the deadly pun of "pall" in "appall." But his critical faculties are proved most clearly in the complete scrapping of the worst three lines of the original poem—lines 4, 12, and 14, all of them loose, sententious, and banal. Their substitutes are firm and hard hitting, stretched taut by the sheer discipline of the form. . . .

"THE BREATHLESS SWING"

The story is told of a student in a creative writing class who claimed: "I've finished a short story. Now I just have to go back over it and put in the symbols." Frost's poems are never like that. His "symbols" are integral, and his poems grow organically, expanding the metaphors logically, assuming direction "from the first line laid down." It was form that created a poem, and this is nowhere more evident than in the strict form of the sonnet. The discipline of form gave Frost his emotional distance from the subject, the distance that he called ulteriority. (He used to quip that he had an "ulteriority complex.") The best description of the way in which form works as a discovery or "clarification" of life, a human victory over the "crudity" of raw material, is given in his own words:

> The most exciting movement in nature is not progress, advance, but expansion and contraction, the opening and shutting of the eye, the hand, the heart, the mind. We throw our arms wide with a gesture of religion to the universe; we close them around a person. We explore and adventure for a while and then we draw in to consolidate our gains. The breathless swing is between subject matter and form.

CHRONOLOGY

1874

Robert Lee, the first child of William and Isabelle (Moodie) Frost, is born on March 26 in San Francisco.

1885

William Frost dies of tuberculosis, leaving family with only eight dollars after funeral expenses; family moves to Lawrence, Massachusetts, to live with relatives.

1889

Frost begins to learn farmwork: tending plants, mowing, sharpening scythes, and reaping.

1890

Oscar Wilde's *Picture of Dorian Gray* is published; William James's *Principles of Psychology* is published; Battle of Wounded Knee.

1891

At Lawrence High, Frost meets and falls in love with fellow student Elinor White; passes preliminary entrance exams for Harvard in Greek, Latin, Greek history, Roman history, algebra, geometry, and English literature.

1892

Becomes engaged to White; enters Dartmouth but leaves after one semester.

1895

Works as a reporter in Lawrence and teaches school; marries Elinor; Freud's *Studies in Hysteria* is published.

1896

Begins writing poetry regularly but feels poems are lacking somehow; son Elliott is born.

1897

Enters Harvard University; Klondike Gold Rush occurs; Bram Stoker's *Dracula* is published.

1899

Withdraws from Harvard; daughter Lesley is born; rents a house and barn in Nethuen, Massachusetts, and begins poultry farming.

1900

Elliott dies of cholera.

1901

Despite his depression, he continues to write poetry every night and also studies botany; Theodore Roosevelt, the Spanish-American War hero, succeeds McKinley as president.

1902

Son Carol is born.

1903

Daughter Marjorie is born.

1905

Takes family to New York City, where his poetry is ignored by editors; daughter Irma is born; Ford Motor Company is founded.

1907

Contracts pneumonia; daughter Elinor is born but lives only one week.

1910

Revises English curriculum for Pinkerton Academy in Derry, New Hampshire; Mark Twain dies.

1911

Moves to Plymouth to teach college education and psychology courses; Marie Curie wins Nobel Prize.

1912

Upset by lack of progress as a poet, moves family to England; *A Boy's Will* is accepted by a London publisher; the *Titanic* sinks.

1913

Attends opening of a bookstore in Kensington, England, where he meets Ezra Pound; Pound favorably reviews *A Boy's Will.*

1914

North of Boston is published; buys farm in Franconia, New Hampshire.

1915

World War I begins; the Frosts return to America.

1916

Mountain Interval is published; Carl Sandburg's *Chicago Poems* is published; first American birth control clinic opens.

1920

Sells Franconia farm and buys one in South Shaftsbury, Vermont; plants orchard with son, Carol.

1921

Begins affiliation with Bread Loaf School of English; Gandhi arrested for civil disobedience.

1923

Selected Poems and *New Hampshire* are published.

1924

Awarded Pulitzer Prize for *New Hampshire.*

1925

Travels extensively, giving lectures and talks; health suffers; Scopes Monkey Trial.

1928

West-Running Brook is published; first television broadcast.

1930

Collected Poems is published.

1931

Wins Pulitzer for *Collected Poems*; Empire State Building is built.

1934

Daughter Marjorie dies; first German concentration camp is erected.

1936

A Further Range is published.

1937

Wins Pulitzer for *A Further Range.*

1938

Elinor dies; Frost collapses and is unable to attend funeral; attends Bread Loaf Writers' Conference; Kathleen Morrison, wife of a Bread Loaf colleague, agrees to be his personal assistant.

1939

World War II begins.

1940

Frost is devastated when Carol commits suicide; F. Scott Fitzgerald dies; John Lennon born.

1942

A Witness Tree is published.

1943

Awarded Pulitzer for *A Witness Tree.*

1945

A Masque of Reason is published; Germany surrenders in World War II; United States drops atomic bombs on Hiroshima and Nagasaki.

1947

Receives a surprise visit from T.S. Eliot; *Steeple Bush* is published.

1949

Complete Poems is published and has record sales.

1959

Appointed to three-year term as the honorary consultant in the humanities at the Library of Congress.

1961

Writes new poem for John F. Kennedy's inauguration but instead recites "The Gift Outright"; Soviet cosmonaut Yuri Gagarin is the first man in space; Bay of Pigs invasion; Berlin Wall is built.

1962

In the Clearing is published; receives presidential and congressional awards; President Kennedy invites Frost to travel to Soviet Union as part of cultural exchange program; wins Bollingen Prize for poetry; Cuban missile crisis.

1963

Dies at midnight on January 29.

FOR FURTHER RESEARCH

WORKS BY ROBERT FROST

Robert Frost, *Collected Poems, Prose, and Plays*. New York: Literary Classics of the United States, 1995.

———, *The Poetry of Robert Frost*. Ed. Edward Connery Lathem. New York: Henry Holt, 1979.

———, *Selected Letters*. Ed. Lawrance Thompson. New York: Holt, 1964.

Robert Frost et al., *Robert Frost: A Tribute to the Source*. New York: Holt, Rinehart, Winston, 1979.

BIOGRAPHIES

Stanley Burnshaw, *Robert Frost Himself*. New York: Braziller, 1986.

Robert Francis, *Robert Frost: A Time to Talk*. Amherst: University of Massachusetts, 1972.

Jeffrey Meyers, *Robert Frost: A Biography*. New York: Houghton Mifflin, 1996.

William H. Pritchard, *Frost: A Literary Life Reconsidered*. New York: Oxford University Press, 1984.

Lawrance Thompson, *Robert Frost: The "Official" Life of the Poet*. 3 vols. New York: Holt, 1988.

LITERARY CRITICISM

Joseph Brodsky, Seamus Heaney, and Derek Walcott, *Homage to Robert Frost*. New York: Farrar, Straus, Giroux, 1996.

Philip Gerber, *Critical Essays on Robert Frost*. Boston: G.K. Hall, 1982.

Randall Jarrell, *Poetry and the Age.* New York: W.W. Norton, 1980.

John Kemp, *Robert Frost and New England: The Poet as Regionalist.* Princeton, NJ: Princeton University Press, 1979.

Edward Connery Lathem, *A Concordance to the Poetry of Robert Frost.* New York: Norton, 1994.

John F. Lynen, *The Pastoral Art of Robert Frost.* New Haven, CT: Yale University Press, 1960.

Theodore Morrison, "The Agitated Heart," *Atlantic Monthly,* July 1967.

George W. Nitchie, *Human Values in the Poetry of Robert Frost.* Durham, NC: Duke University Press, 1960.

Richard Poirier and John Hollander, *Robert Frost: The Work of Knowing.* Palo Alto, CA: Stanford University Press, 1990.

HISTORICAL BACKGROUND

Frank Lentricchia, *Robert Frost: Modern Poetics and the Landscape of Self.* Durham, NC: Duke University Press, 1975.

RELATED WEBSITE

Sarah R. Jackson, *Frost in Cyberspace.* Available at http://www.libarts.sfasu.edu/frost/frost.html.

INDEX